OUTNUMBERED

Chronicles of a Manhattan Conservative

Jedediah Bila

ISBN-13: 978-0-9835768-0-8

DISCLAIMER: This book is based on actual events and
conversations, with the caveat that I have done some minor
editing and omitted certain details (such as names, exact
locations) out of consideration for the people and/or entities
described. In addition, the quotes in this book are not
verbatim. In most instances, conversations and incidents that
are depicted were reconstructed from contemporaneous
notes memorialized shortly after their occurrence. All quotes
are intended to capture the substance or spirit of the
statements made or the distilled essence of what was stated to
me. They are not intended to be, and should not be
understood to be, a literal reiteration of any conversation or
attributed to any specific individual.

To my parents, Solange and Tony, who taught me to reach high, stand tall, and always be true to my heart.

CONTENTS

I. *Introduction*: Plain Old Everyday Life........................ 1

II. Conservative Girl with a Twist..................................... 5

III. Just a New York Girl ... with a Palin Pin

      • *October 2008* 9

      • *November 2008*... 28

      • *December 2008*.. 62

      • *January 2009*.. 82

      • *February 2009*... 106

      • *March 2009*... 129

IV. Old Buddy, Old Pal and Schoolhouse Grace......... 137

V. Epilogue... 143

VI. Acknowledgments... 149

VII. Photo Gallery: Emma Bila... 153

VIII. About the Author... 159

I.

Introduction:

PLAIN OLD EVERYDAY LIFE

I remember sitting at my grandparents' kitchen table one March afternoon during my sophomore year of high school. I was reading over an essay I'd just written for English class, getting more and more frustrated by the second. It just wasn't hitting home.

My grandfather had volunteered to read it over and give me his opinion. Poppy could always be counted on for two things— blunt honesty and some of the best marinara sauce this world has ever tasted.

"It's missing something, right?" I asked when he had finished. He lowered his glasses, took a deep breath, and leaned in as he always did when getting ready to give me advice.

"It's missing the part that makes me want to walk those steps with you, open my eyes, and look around," he said. I remember trying as best as I could to visualize what he meant. He continued, "Sometimes it's the stuff that happens in plain old everyday life—the realness of it all—that speaks the biggest truths."

I've never lost sight of those words. In fact, that March afternoon, I took a piece of my grandfather's advice and began writing journal entries that would help me to reflect on the meaning of everything going on around me. And he was right—they have always felt honest … and authentic … and, being the private person that I am, a little scary to put down on paper. But they have helped me to discover what perhaps I might never have seen.

In October of 2008, in the midst of one of the most passionate election seasons I've witnessed thus far, I began a different kind of journal. After a few interesting Manhattan encounters—the details of which I recorded on napkins, loose-leaf paper, or whatever I could snatch from my bag at the time—I saw a thematic pattern developing. I found myself jotting down conversations as they occurred on the subway, in the private school where I was a teacher and tenth-grade Dean, and in other locations. I'd later write up reflective commentary on what had transpired. And I quickly found myself talking to a reader—to someone walking beside me on the journey with whom I could share my thoughts and experiences—as I often do in my written reflections.

It wasn't until recently, after I'd embarked upon a new voyage as a conservative columnist and commentator, that I sat down and read my October of 2008 to March of 2009 reflections as a whole. I realized that I had something I wanted to share.

The world of politics had emerged through the "plain old everyday life" my grandfather talked about seventeen years ago. The voices of regular people in this great big city that rarely sleeps embody a substance that no statistic, fancy fact, or intellectual treatise ever could. And the truths that those voices brought to life have transcended the months featured in this text, as they're still alive and well this May of 2011.

I invite you to venture with me throughout my days and nights between October of 2008 and March of 2009. You'll join me as I hit the gym, had a bite out to eat with friends, talked to students and administrators, sampled the party scene, and more. You'll get a sense of how I see this very big, yet very small city around me, and how it sees me.

You'll also get a peek into my post-March of 2009 world. How has my life changed, and how did many in my far-left circle begin to see this regular Manhattan conservative when I hit their living room TVs?

Most importantly, you'll witness themes like the conservative versus liberal world view, elitism, "feminism" versus feminism, intolerance, and "diversity," all brought to life by regular New Yorkers. With the exception of some minor editing, the integrity of my original written reflections has been maintained.

As we gear up for the intensity that's sure to embody America's 2012 presidential election, perhaps the real-life journey you'll find on these pages will lead you to look at yourself, at politics, and at those around you with a brand new gaze. And so I bring you something unconventional, something I hope will make you want to walk those steps with me, open your eyes, and look around.

II.

CONSERVATIVE GIRL WITH A TWIST

Hello, America. My name is Jedediah Bila and I'm a Manhattan conservative.

Before we get started, I thought I'd give you a little insight into who I am, especially because I've already told you I'm a conservative and you're likely picturing me writing this while wearing the fur of a once-cuddly animal, holding a rifle in one hand and the Bible in the other, singing verses of "The Star-Spangled Banner" as I pencil my $50,000 bonus into my checkbook, make a mental note to purchase a six-pack of aerosol spray cans, and wonder why Lincoln had such a problem with slavery.

Well, let's just say you might be a *little* off.

I grew up mostly in Staten Island, currently live in Midtown Manhattan, and earned a Master of Arts degree from Columbia

University in Spanish literature. I worked my butt off at a small liberal arts college—Wagner College—because I knew that a full scholarship was my only ticket to the program I had my eye on. There was just no way my parents were affording tuition of over $40,000 a year.

My graduate thesis was titled "Confinement Within a Patriarchal Cell: Unmasking Female Liberty in Galdos's *Fortunata y Jacinta.*" A classmate insisted that a conservative was "unfit" to explore such a topic.

When I was a teenager, I thought I wanted to become an actress, but I hurried home after my first audition to write a journal entry on the objectification of women in the television industry. When I revisited the acting bug in my early twenties, I knew something was wrong when I began only auditioning for roles I could feature in post-graduate writings on the female psyche. I even dressed up in a nurse's costume once and took part in a spoof on the porn industry—no nudity or touching, of course. I have to admit that I sometimes wish I'd stayed in the business long enough to punch out the first casting director to ask me if I'd take my clothes off for a role. Damn, that would've made a great essay.

I'm an animal lover. I've probably rescued more stray cats than the ASPCA. Three of them reside in my parents' home in Staten Island.

I eat like a champ. No beef, veal, lamb, or pork, though. On many days, I'm the perfect vegan.

The kitchen and I don't get along too well. Luckily, some of my best friends are cooking gurus. Most of my food is organic, and I often carry a reusable tote to Whole Foods.

My favorite musician is Sarah McLachlan. My good friend, a lesbian, says Sarah's music is "too gay" for her. "Not possible," I usually answer before we sit down to watch a girl try to claw her way out of a tin box in the latest horror flick.

I went to Catholic school on Staten Island for twelve years, and sometime around college was probably the last time I attended Mass. With that being said, God is the last person I talk to each night before bed. I just discovered at some point that for me, heart to hearts beside my nightstand felt more right.

From September of 2006 until June of 2010, I taught Spanish at a Manhattan private school. I was also a Student Adviser and tenth-grade Dean there.

I began writing political columns regularly in March of 2009 because, once again, it just felt right. I tend to follow my heart without thinking sometimes. It hasn't betrayed me thus far.

Oh, and I love fitness. I'll pass on the Pilates and Yoga, but I'll gladly meet you in the weight room or the boxing ring. Your size and strength won't intimidate me. My speed and endurance may intimidate *you*. Don't worry, I'll shake your hand in the end and wish you better luck next time.

So, there you have it. That's what this Manhattan conservative looks like. I can already hear the chants on the left of "No, she's on the wrong side! She carries a reusable tote!" A quick glance at my M.A. thesis title and the National Organization for Women will be recruiting me for conservative rehab meetings. But I assure you, I *am* a conservative. And although the word gets tossed around these days as much as energy shots at Equinox, it still means something to me. So, here's why I call myself conservative:

I believe in liberty ... as in the freedom to choose whether or not you want health insurance.

I believe in opportunity. I like government small, taxes low, and incentive high.

I believe in a strong national defense. All the health care debates in the world won't mean much if we don't have a country.

I believe in personal responsibility. I own my choices. See it, want it, seize it.

I believe in the second amendment. The only person who can really be trusted to protect you at the end of the day is you.

I believe in the sanctity of life. That includes the unborn, who will one day be our leaders.

I'm also not afraid of the "C" word. You know, Constitution.

Now that you have a sense of me and the principles that guide me, we're ready to begin. So, come walk with me ...

III.

JUST A NEW YORK GIRL ...
WITH A PALIN PIN

October 2008

* * * * *

The subway came late today. And to top it all off, the heel of my left pump broke when I slipped on saran wrap on the landing. So, I spent the rest of the day about an inch taller on the right side. Hey, at least it was the right, you know?

My typical ride to school is about ten minutes, but this morning the train decided to take a nap at 68th Street, so ten turned into twenty pretty quickly. And what an interesting twenty it was.

"Racist," a woman muttered across the aisle, and I lifted my stare to see who she was talking to. To my surprise, she was looking at me. Perhaps *glaring* is a more fitting word.

"Huh?" I asked.

"What are you, dumb or something?" an older woman sitting beside her added.

"I'm sorry, but I think you might have the wrong person," I replied.

"Your pin, dummy. Do you ban books, too?" the younger woman asked. I looked down at the small "Palin Power" pin that sat on the strap of my briefcase. I couldn't help myself and began to laugh, probably not the best response considering I now had several angry New Yorkers peering back and forth from the pin to my face. The doors opened and the two women stood to exit.

"I hope you and that idiot know you're going to lose," the older lady said as she stepped onto the platform.

"Yes we can, bitch!" the other exclaimed, and a few passengers laughed. I noticed several "Change" pins, one of which featured a picture of Barack Obama with a halo above his head. I could tell from the construction paper that it was hand-made.

With one stop left to go, I snatched my iPod from my bag. I hit play and Sarah McLachlan's "Full of Grace" began. Just before I exited the train, my eyes caught a glimpse of a sheet of loose-leaf paper resting beneath a nearby seat. On the top was written, "New York City: Home of Tolerance and Diversity." *Gee*, I thought. *I wonder if those ladies left it behind.*

The rest of the day went along as usual. Bush-bashing jokes and intermittent chitchat about the horrors of global warming were the imperfect background to my lunch in the faculty room. I closed the school day with plenty of verb conjugations and capped off my night correcting exams, re-reading *The Great Gatsby*, and catching up on the latest headlines. Oh, and with a trip to the gym for some one-on-one time with a spin bike I named Slick Willie because its pedals seem to move faster than the rest.

* * * * *

"Ms. Bila's *definitely* a Republican," said one of my students as he entered class this morning.

"What?" I asked.

"She has Captain America as her computer background!" he exclaimed to a friend. It was true. Captain America is one of my favorite superheroes, second only to Peter Parker *before* he turns into Spider-Man. What can I say? Nerdy vulnerability has always made me weak in the knees.

"Oh my God," said a female student. "Ms. Bila, you're obsessed with America."

"Not obsessed. But it is our country, right?" I replied with a smile.

"She must have a poster of George Bush above her bed," said a boy.

"And guns. Lots of guns," added another.

"And look, there's an American flag poster on our wall! Oh my God!" shouted the young gentleman who had been the first to notice my Captain America computer wallpaper.

"Ms. Bila, that's too much," said a girl. "Way over the top with the America stuff." I couldn't help but wonder at what point in our history things had gone so terribly wrong to cause kids to think that an American flag poster and a computer background of Captain America were "over the top."

I spent the rest of class conjugating irregular verbs and reviewing idiomatic expressions. In fact, that's essentially what I did for the remainder of the day. However, I couldn't get my students' comments from this morning out of my head.

I began to think about the students I've taught over the years. In so many cases, there seemed to be no innate love of country, no appreciation for the opportunity America had afforded their parents, enabling them to send their children to prestigious schools. Aside from what kind of leaders those kids would become, what kind would they elect? Would they *hope* for a candidate who would likely spend more time apologizing for America than saluting her? Would that be the *change they would believe in*?

Ms. Bila's definitely a Republican echoed through my mind as I exited the train and began my walk home. If American flags and patriotism were synonymous in their minds with the word "Republican," what exactly did they think of Democrats? One of my self-proclaimed liberal Democrat friends—a thirty-six-year-old native Manhattanite—answered that question for me before dinner tonight.

"We liberals just aren't like that when it comes to America," she said. "I mean, we're not the only country in the world, you know?" I paused as I stood over my freshly-cooked—or shall I say, freshly-burnt— veggies. She added, "If I saw some girl walking around New York City with an American flag pin, I'd know right away that she was a lonely Republican."

I had never been so proud to be a lonely Republican in New York City.

* * * * *

I only passed two pro-Obama stands on my way to Whole Foods today. The weather must have gotten to the third and fourth. The shirts that read "Barack Obama Is My Homeboy" seemed to grab most of the attention.

I arrived at spin class a few minutes late, thanks to a debate between a customer and a cashier at Whole Foods over what the price of two bundles of kale *should* be. Luckily, my favorite bike—Slick Willie—hadn't been swept up by another. Not too many people were ever eager to be front and center at spin, so Slick Willie and I enjoyed a fairly monogamous relationship. There was that one occasional out-of-town blonde, though.

"Sometimes I can't believe how dumb the rest of the country is," said a girl to a friend. "Sarah Palin is like the stupidest woman you could possibly find."

"Really? You think so?" I interjected with a grin.

"Republicans are all the same," she said. "They're just the worst kind of people."

"Don't forget animal-haters," I said with a wink.

"Yeah, that too!" she replied with a smile. She missed my sarcasm. It made it all the funnier.

"Are you a Democrat?" I asked.

"Of course," she replied.

"Why?" My tone was nondescript. "Why are you a Democrat and not a Republican?"

"Democrats help people in need. Republicans rob people in need." Had she stolen that from the DNC website?

"Aaah, ok," I said as I tried not to crack a smile.

The class seemed more exhausting than usual, but I loved every minute. It's strange, but I find a little piece of myself every time I push my body past where I thought it could go. My high school track coach used to tell us before every race, "A strong mind builds a strong body." Life has taught me that a strong body also builds a strong mind.

Spin class ended about five minutes early, as a young lady in the third row whom I knew from a few other classes slipped off her bike and fell. She thankfully wasn't injured. As several of us gathered around her to assure that she was okay, I caught a glimpse of the Republican-hater whom I had spoken with earlier. She was busy finishing off her workout despite the commotion.

What was that she had said again? Oh, right. *Democrats help people in need.*

* * * * *

I went downtown today to visit the site of the fallen Twin Towers. I stood outside for some time just looking ahead … remembering … missing the way they used to stretch up into the sky like they knew there was something incredible just out of reach. It's rare when I head down there, to be completely honest. I've never quite been able to get the sound of that plane overhead out of my mind, or the image of those poor people waving items out of windows with the hope that someone would come to their rescue.

I was working at an insurance company in September of 2001, my first job out of grad school. Our offices were in One Liberty Plaza, right across the street from the World Trade Center. I was at my desk when the first plane struck the North Tower and stepped outside my lobby just as the South Tower was hit. I ran for my life right along with everyone else.

I spent the afternoon in a stranger's apartment watching the news, a refuge from the chaos of the streets and a place to clean up my cuts and wash the soot from my eyes. I remember that political parties didn't matter that day. We were all in it together.

It's amazing how terribly flawed humanity is that it takes such tragedy to remind us that we're all still people.

I got home around 4:00 p.m. on September 11, 2001, after walking across the Manhattan Bridge and catching a ride to Staten Island with a family friend. I didn't find out until hours later that I had missed a memo from my boss asking me to deliver a package to a meeting in the North Tower at 8:45 a.m. The tower had been struck at 8:46. It was at that moment I promised myself that I'd never spend a day of my life doing something that didn't make me feel alive.

Tonight I sit with a heavy heart, so many emotions from that indelible morning in 2001 still so accessible. I still feel so helpless when I think of those trapped people. And I'm still so angry that evil got to do a victory lap. I don't know what God would say about that, but I wish I could somehow understand why He didn't jump in and scoop those people up. On second thought, maybe He did.

I called a college friend after dinner tonight to vent, but all she wanted to talk about was how she thought President Bush had sat in that Florida second-grade classroom too long.

"Do you remember the video of that moron just sitting there in a daze?" she asked. "You know, the sooner you realize what an idiot he is, the sooner you can get on my team."

I didn't say anything. No witty comeback, no sharp retort. Just silence in memory of the day when there weren't any teams.

* * * * *

"Excuse me, Miss, but do you have a minute for Planned Parenthood?" asked a woman with a clipboard on Third Avenue this morning. *I have a minute to help defund it*, I thought as I hit the subway stairs.

I spent a good part of the morning struggling to keep my eyes open, as a couple on my floor had spent the better part of the prior night cursing, screaming, and wishing each other dead. At one point, a loud thump jolted me out of a rather pleasant dream. At another, I was horrified by a twenty-second patch of silence, hoping that one hadn't chucked the other out the window. *Nah*, I thought. *It's only the second floor. What would be the point?*

Lunch couldn't come quickly enough, as I had skipped my usual seven-grain muffin and strawberry-kale smoothie in the a.m. (I know, it's no bacon, egg, and cheese) and my stomach was in full rebellion. Guacamole, salad, beans, and granola never tasted so good. Despite the rowdiness of nearby middle schoolers, I was just too content with my food—and with my draft of an essay on feminism—to be in the least bit bothered.

"She's just not fit to serve," said a male teacher at a faculty table to my right.

"That's the understatement of the year," said a female teacher. "The woman is an idiot."

"McCain seems like a stand-up kind of guy," said another.

"Well, he's not the worst of them, that's for sure. But that airhead from Alaska has got to go," another added.

"She should be at home with her kids. What kind of a mother leaves her five kids at home to run for office?" asked one of the gentlemen. I nearly choked on my juice. *What kind of a mother leaves her five kids at home to run for office?* Had I been teleported to 1920 and didn't know it? I looked up and awaited a response from one of the three female teachers seated at the table. Not one said a word. Proud members of the National Organization for Women?

"Regardless, she's totally incompetent. No experience whatsoever," one of the women finally added after a prolonged silence. *I guess that running a business, a city, and a state doesn't count,* I thought.

The rest of the day went by pretty quickly, and I found myself writing for much of the night. I did get in a quick run, though, and downed three bowls of escarole and beans. I couldn't seem to forget what that teacher had said at lunch this afternoon. *What kind of a mother leaves her five kids at home to run for office?* Interesting commentary from a self-proclaimed liberal. You know, the avant-garde, need-to-teach-conservatives-a-thing-or-two-about-modernity kind.

* * * * *

"Psst!" I heard from the right. I looked around, but didn't see anyone. "Psst!" I turned again, and this time an adorable old lady—she had to be at least eighty, if not more—was wide-eyed and pointing frantically at her collar, then gesturing toward mine. I jumped about a foot in the air, convinced that some grotesque bug was on its way toward my face. I looked down and saw nothing.

"You might want to cover that up," she whispered as she tucked my Palin pin inside my outer jacket. "I don't want you getting yourself killed now, young lady," she added.

"Oh, it's okay. I haven't been beaten up yet," I said with a laugh.

"Please be careful," she replied. "I nearly got knocked to the ground because of one of those a few weeks ago. It's just not worth the fight, you know?" As I watched her exit the deli, I stood wondering what in heaven's name had possessed someone to nearly knock down a barely five-foot, eighty-something-year-old woman because of a pin. Where in the hell am I living?

I sat for a little while, staring out the window at Lexington Avenue, observing the physical diversity of people who passed by. Did so many of them look different on the outside, but think the same? I wondered if any had hidden their Palin pins, too. *It's just not worth the fight* ran through my mind. I lifted the pin out of my jacket. *If people don't fight, there will be nothing left to fight for*, I thought.

I decided to walk home and, to no surprise, faced my fair share of grimaces and comments. A woman mumbled "Ignorant bitch" as I rounded Third Avenue. A man stopped me to "inform" me that if I wanted to support hatred, I "should move to a place like Utah." A teenager told me to "get the hell out of Obama's city." But one mom carrying an infant gave me a thumbs up, and that made it all worthwhile.

Of course, when I told my mom what had happened, she was terrified. Her desire to protect her little girl would always take precedence over any freedom of speech crusade. I promised I'd spend two hours each week in the boxing ring. She wasn't amused.

Dad gave me a stern "Be careful" lecture on the phone after dinner, but I could sense the pride swelling in his voice. There was no way Tony Bila would ever tell me to take that pin off. During my time at Columbia University, he had parked outside repeatedly with an enormous Rush Limbaugh sticker across his rear bumper. Now *that's* guts.

It's close to 1:00 a.m., and soon I'll be heading to bed. I just sifted through some media commentary on how Sarah Palin is the anti-feminist. Someone needs to set that record straight … for the girls who will otherwise grow up thinking that feminism and abortion must go hand in hand. Because they deserve better.

* * * * *

"I can't believe that girl's cousin is pregnant," said a college student from my neighborhood on the subway this morning. Her friends continued:

"I know. She's freaking out."

"Why? She should just get an abortion."

"I know, right. That's what I told her." *Not your place to have this talk*, I thought to myself. The girl whom I knew looked over at me.

"I just hope she gets the guidance she needs," I interjected.

"Oh, she'll be fine. I think it's a quick pill or something like that," a boy said. *Not your place to have this talk.*

"I hope that whoever is guiding her helps her to explore her options," I said.

"Options? I would've downed that pill the second I found out," added a girl. They began to laugh. *Not your place to have this talk.*

"It's not quite so simple," I said.

"Sounds simple to me," added a guy nonchalantly. Somehow, somewhere, they had come to believe that pregnancy was something that could be quickly "fixed" with an off-the-cuff shrug and a vitamin-like tablet.

"You okay?" asked one of the girls as she glanced at me. I guess I hadn't hidden my sadness too well.

"Yeah, fine."

"Don't worry," she said. "The girl who's pregnant is headed to Planned Parenthood for some help today." My stomach sank. The doors opened and they exited.

I spent the rest of the afternoon disgusted with myself. Although it was an awkward setting and I barely knew them, I had missed the chance to educate those kids about what I thought Planned Parenthood's "help" was sure to look like. I had let them down, and I knew it.

Tonight I went to a costume party at a friend's house in Soho. My friend was Little Red Riding Hood and I was the wolf. There were at least three Obamas, one of whom was half Obama and half Clark Kent, with a superman outfit showing underneath. There was one Sarah Palin wearing a "Kick Me" sign on her back. At one point, all of the Obamas started a "hope and change" song. A guy dressed as a Cabbage Patch Kid—awesome costume—chimed in.

"Hope for what?" I asked when things had quieted down. A bunch of people turned to look at me. "I'm just wondering … hope for what? Change how?" They quickly shifted their focus to a woman dressed as a carton of milk.

I gathered my belongings a few minutes later, wiped out from an early start this morning. As I walked through the kitchen toward the front door, I overheard the Cabbage Patch Kid whispering to a friend, King Kong: "Wait, though. All kidding aside, hope for *what*?" King Kong shrugged. They both looked puzzled. I guess someone had heard me after all.

November 2008

* * * * *

I went to vote bright and early this morning. When I hit the line, there were about twenty people ahead of me. Here's a sample of what I heard while waiting:

"I can't wait. This guy's gonna change *everything*."

"It's like God knew we needed something and sent it to us."

"The old dude's going down. And he's taking that dumbass beauty queen with him."

"Yes we will! New York for Obama!"

That last one was followed by a "New York for Obama" chant. Two people weren't singing. One was me.

I exited the voting booth and felt alive. There was no doubt which way the New York results would go, but there was something so empowering about pulling that lever. Why would anyone be a silent bystander when the ability to take a stand is so accessible? I didn't get it. Have some Americans become so spoiled that having the power to shape the country we live in no longer has meaning?

I arrived at school shortly after. We had a dress down day and we all got to wear red, white, and blue. I opted for a navy blue hoodie with military patches. I was the proud owner of a handful of glares within the first five minutes.

My school was a sea of Obama blue. Pins and logo t-shirts flooded the auditorium. A student talked about how everyone who was eligible to vote needed to get out and do so, about how the election could *change* the face of politics forever, and about how she had so much *hope* for the future.

"So, how many of you would vote for Obama today if you could?" she asked. A flood of hands instantly rose. *Wow*, I thought. *You'd think she just asked who wanted an endless supply of free candy.* A quick glance to the back of the room revealed that every teacher whom I could see had also raised his or her hand.

"Okay now, who would vote for McCain?" About five or six students slowly lifted their arms. They looked terrified. Some of their classmates began to giggle. I quickly raised my hand as well. Here's a taste of the comments that followed:

"Ms. Bila! What? You're a Republican?" The boy looked horrified. He clutched his Obama pin in distress. *Relax*, I thought. *I mean, it's not like I'd just spent the afternoon with … oh, I don't know … an unrepentant terrorist.*

"Don't you want change? Obama's the coolest guy ever. And McCain picked that nutcase from Alaska," another whispered. *That "nutcase" from Alaska is the reason he got my vote*, I thought as I smiled.

An administrator went on to talk about how he's a Democrat and how the candidates he votes for typically win because "New York is a Democrat state." He wondered aloud what it must be like to live in a place where "you're sort of the odd man out."

I didn't say a word, but a part of me wishes I had. I wish I'd told him that there are definitely times I wish I was voting in a place where my chosen candidates often had a good shot of winning, but there's something kind of special about being different. Walking through the city with my Palin pin fastened to my jacket and my head held high is building me up on the inside. And a part of me is really grateful for that.

A few hours later, I would get some unsought advice from a seventeen-year-old whom I was helping with homework. "You know, you, of all people, should be on Obama's side," she said.

"Why is that?" I asked.

"Because he's all about propping up the little people. You know, the ones who don't make a lot of money and stuff." I began laughing. I guess I had never thought of myself as a "little person" before. I knew that her parents were big Obama supporters and decided that a brief statement on the falsehood of the "Obama, hero of the common folk" motif would suffice.

She went on to state that America is "too cocky" and that "the land of opportunity is a big farce," all the while sipping Evian from the second floor of her mother's duplex on the Upper West Side.

My friend Andy and I watched the election returns roll in from my apartment, and neither of us was too surprised. New York was called within the usual few minutes of the polls closing. I have to admit that I would've liked to have heard something from Palin. She didn't speak, but she certainly looked like she wanted to. In fact, she looked like she had a lot left to say.

I'm headed to bed now. I hope that Barack Obama will be closer to the hope he has talked so much about than the change his voting record represents. I guess we'll find out soon enough.

* * * * *

Last night I received an excited post-election email from a teacher at my school. She had sent it to many of us. Her assumption that we were all celebrating the election's outcome was astounding to me. Here is some of the dialogue I heard today in the faculty room:

"I'm so happy! I could hardly contain myself last night."

"The world seems so content. I'm just glad people won't hate America so much anymore."

"Finally, a president who can read again."

Several front pages of newspapers were stapled on administration billboards. In the hallways, some teachers were discussing a newfound hope for the country with their students. I spent most of the day grading exams, teaching a medley of verb tenses, and writing an essay on collectivism. Hmmm, I can't imagine what inspired that topic.

Here's a taste of the comments my students had for me:

"Ms. Bila, you must be way depressed that she's headed back to see Russia from her house."

"Tina Fey?" I asked. They looked puzzled. "After all, that's who said that, right?" They didn't get it.

"Come on, Ms. Bila, a Harvard president. That's what America needs." I didn't respond. He continued, "Well then, what do *you* think America needs?"

"I think America needs someone who understands the gift of being an American," I answered.

They looked confused. One kid said "Huh?" I returned to verb conjugations.

Tonight I got a call from a friend who hadn't returned my last few phone calls. It turns out she was offended by the pro-liberty, pro-Constitution images and status updates on my Facebook page. She called to say she was sorry and that she should've let me know what was up sooner.

"What exactly were you offended by?" I asked. She revealed that my pro-legal immigration/anti-illegal immigration and pro-Palin posts were of particular distaste. Oh, and that one update that read, "New York City: hub of intellectual diversity or Brave New World?"

"But I wasn't attacking you personally," I said.

"I know. I guess it's just that everyone around me was so excited after the election. Everyone around me … everyone … saw it the same way. We all think the same, we all see it the same, we all couldn't wait for him to win. And then there's you. You're just so … different." I forgave her, but I knew that a real

33

friendship could never exist if my opinions wouldn't have a place in it.

We all think the same, we all see it the same, we all couldn't wait for him to win echoed through my mind. New York City: hub of intellectual diversity or Brave New World?

* * * * *

"I really don't get what the big deal is."

"The big deal is that Republicans make a big deal out of everything."

"I mean, I'm not saying she should've been so bold, but she was telling the truth."

I was at a restaurant on the Upper East Side having dinner with some acquaintances. We were discussing a teacher who had inserted her liberal opinion into a lesson—namely, her distaste for Ronald Reagan.

"How can you not think that's a big deal?" I asked. "Kids are supposed to go to school to learn *how* to think, not *what* to think."

"I disagree in a sense," said one of the ladies. "If you know something is outright wrong, isn't it your job to inform kids?"

"Yeah, to help them see the problems in the world that you see," another added.

"It's not your job to teach your opinion," I said. "It's your job to help kids develop their own."

"Yeah, but look at Iraq, for example. It's a totally senseless war," a gentleman said. "I have no issue with any teacher educating students on that."

"I agree," said another. They were all New York City teachers. Three worked in the public school system—two in high schools and one in a middle school. The fourth was a university professor.

"That's not education," I replied. "That's called putting your opinion out there and labeling it as truth. If that's your goal, you should probably quit your jobs. You'd all have promising futures in 'objective' media." They didn't reply. Within seconds, they had shifted over to an in-depth discussion about whether the West Side or East Side of Manhattan is more likable.

I spent tonight thinking about my education. I feel blessed to have gone to a high school where I was encouraged to develop my own opinion. In fact, I had one history teacher back then who I still think is one of the smartest women I've ever met. Her tilt to the left was no secret—there were hints here and there for sure—but I never felt that it wasn't okay to see things differently. In fact, she often patted me on the back for thinking long and hard enough to draw my own conclusions. I know now that she was a rare gift so many kids don't get to experience.

A few years after earning my Master of Arts degree, I took a job doing some adjunct teaching at a college. It was after I had parted ways with my Ph.D. program, as the subject matter didn't inspire me nearly enough for an extra four-year commitment.

I remember being asked to remove patriotic displays from outside the door of the teacher's office I was temporarily housed in. Several of them read "Support Our Troops," a couple more read "God Bless America," and there were two references to "freedom fries" with the McDonald's logo. The professor who had lent me her office called me and asked me to take them down. She said that they were inspiring too much controversy and that a teacher in the foreign language department needed to act like one. I remember tearing the last one off, turning around, and glancing at the door of a fellow foreign language professor. There were at least two anti-war slogans and a couple of Bush jokes.

Lesson of the day: In the educational system, your opinion *does* matter. Just make sure it's academia-approved.

* * * * *

"What's that pin for, Ms. B?" one of my students asked me this morning. "That's not the usual one you wear." She was right. My "usual one" was a small American flag. Today's was a soldier saluting.

"It's a tribute to our veterans," I answered.

"Why?"

"Because it's Veterans Day," I replied.

"What's that?" she asked. I went on to explain the day's meaning. I couldn't help but be concerned that someone hadn't done so already. It reminded me of the time last year when I was hanging a poster on my classroom's back wall of the Pledge of Allegiance. Only a couple of students in the room could recite it. They told me that they had learned it in kindergarten, but it had been a long time ago. It had broken my heart. The future leaders of our country are well-versed in Al Gore's convenient untruths, but don't know that we are "one nation under God." Where will that take us?

During my lunch break, I sat next to a young couple feasting on burgers and fries at a café. "I need to lose weight," the woman said to her husband or boyfriend in an exasperated voice. He shrugged. "I'm thinking of joining this program where you hire someone to monitor what you eat for a month. They tell you what food to buy, clear out your fridge, and show up at the house for random checks." *Food police?* I thought. *Was that like a culinary mob?*

"Why?" her companion asked.

"Because I need to lose weight," she repeated. "It's way too hard to do it myself. I'm addicted to carbs." He started laughing. "It's not funny, Mark. I have a serious carb addiction." I have no idea how that guy kept a straight face.

"I'm sorry," he answered.

"Whatever. I need someone to take the bull by the horns." *Note to self,* I thought. *If I'm ever in need of a job, invent something stupid and preach to the lazy about how much they need me.*

The woman went on reading *The New York Times*, insisting that Obama is gearing up to save the country. *But will he save the chubby* almost slipped through my lips. Good thing for a mouthful of cantaloupe.

The rest of the day and night were pretty uneventful. I went for a long run in the park and sifted through the news after dinner. I was still getting a kick out of that woman in the café. I've never understood the desire for someone to do for you what you can and should do for yourself.

I remember the Christmas my friend bought me three personal training sessions at a local gym. I used the first one, but was beside myself watching the trainer bring me my weights, adjust my bars, and toss me a ball I could've easily bounced off a wall myself. I remember her telling me to stop doing more reps than she asked for, that my "one-two-three" counts were drowning out hers, and that I should relax a bit and let her do her job. Relax? At the gym? I don't think so.

At the end of the day, you've got to run the race like no one's setting your pace beside you. It's clear to me that the woman I sat next to in the café today—at her core—is so different from me. Kind of interesting that our politics are equally divergent, no? I'll leave the rest of that equation to you.

* * * * *

I ran into an old friend this afternoon. I was on my lunch
break and he was headed to a job interview.

"So, I hear you're a big Palinista," he said.

"As in I voted for Palin?" I asked.

"No, as in you actually think she has a brain."

"Oh, well then yes, I guess that makes me a Palinista," I
replied.

"A friend of mine is on your Facebook page. Says you sound
like you swallowed a Reagan pill or something." *Reagan pill,* I
thought. *What a great gift for Barack Obama.*

"You know me. I've always been a power-to-the-people kind
of girl."

"I know," he said with an eye roll. "I guess you just didn't
really talk about that stuff in college." He was right. I had been
very engaged in politics in high school. I remember darting
through the halls hanging posters for George H. W. Bush. I
began wondering why members of certain women's groups
whom I encountered through friends seemed to hate it every
time I talked about the sanctity of life. And I tried to engage my

41

buddies in discussions about abortion, taxes, and gun rights. My friends were quick to tell me when I was being a pain in the ass. I'd usually follow that up with one last comment about how lucky we were to live in a place where I could annoy everyone with my First Amendment right to spew political commentary.

When I started college, I decided I wanted to do things differently. I felt drawn to psychology and art history. I wanted to study new things. I remember thinking, *It's time to put my politics aside and open different doors.* And that's precisely what I thought I did.

On paper, I didn't have much to say about the political scene in those four years. I didn't show up every morning with a copy of *The Wall Street Journal* or research governors and mayors across America who I thought might be on their way to the top. But my values never left me.

I found myself drawn to literary characters who weren't defined by the lives they'd been handed, but by the ones they had made for themselves. Themes of self-sufficiency, personal responsibility, and the need to free yourself from the crutches of your past in order to make the most of your future stood out for me in readings. I picked psychology professors who discouraged drugs as a form of treatment, and instead encouraged therapy where you'd have to do hard work to find your own answers. I felt empowered by reading about entrepreneurship and was perturbed by economic theories that aimed to equalize, rather than to encourage the best and brightest to rise to the top.

"You're right," I said to my friend as I smiled. "I didn't talk about it much in college. But sometimes it's what you carry on the inside that counts."

"You'll come around, lady. It's the year of change." He didn't quite get it. That was okay with me.

When I made the decision to step back from politics in 1996, I was worried that one day I'd regret it. I have to admit that I don't. I look back at college as a time when I discovered so much of the world I had never seen—and found the best part of me. I learned how to love and who to trust. I learned that what people say about you has a lot more to do with them than with you. I learned that there will always be people who love you, people who hate you, and those who can't make up their minds. None of that is a reason to stop being who you are. Most of all, I learned that the things on the inside that guide you, the ones that help you to choose right from wrong, to take that leap or not, to turn right or left … they are a part of everything you do. Even if you divert your gaze, they stick with you.

I picked up *The Wall Street Journal* in September of 2000 and engaged in a lengthy debate with a friend about fiscal responsibility. I didn't feel like I was coming back home. I had been there all along.

* * * * *

I spent some time at the Union Square dog park this afternoon. There's just something about watching animals tackle each other in the dirt that makes me smile. There weren't too many pups out and about, but the ones that were had quite a bit of spunk. I've been toying with the idea of getting a dog for months—something small and fluffy. I love big dogs, too, but there's something about a Rottweiler in a five-hundred-square-foot apartment that doesn't seem quite right.

"Oreo, run boy!" a woman shouted to a small black and white mutt as she tossed a ball and he dove head first to retrieve it. I instantly fell in love with him. He was mischievous, klutzy, and fearless. And you could tell that he was a big softy with lots of cuddle power. I had no doubt he'd make a fine best friend.

In no time at all, Oreo had found a playmate in a chocolate toy poodle. She was sassy, a bit of a princess, and strutted with her snout held high. She'd glance over at him every now and then to make sure he was looking her way. She was adorable, but far too afraid of getting her paws dirty for my taste.

Soon enough, Oreo and Chloe—that was her name—were all over each other. She'd nibble at his ear, he'd playfully dash away, and she'd coyly invite him closer with a hop, a skip, and a jump. Chloe's owner sat on a bench beside me.

"Oreo, come here!" his owner shouted. Her eyes were wide and cheeks flushed. "Oreo, now!" she insisted. Oreo looked confused. His little head jolted back and forth from his mom to his newfound crush. "I said now!"

Chloe's owner looked perplexed as Oreo approached his mom with his head down. He looked like he'd just lost his best pal. "Sorry, kiddo, but that pup's just not for you," she said as she glared at Chloe's mom.

"Ummm, is there a problem?" Chloe's owner asked.

"No, no problem," Oreo's mom replied curtly. "Where'd you get that shirt for her, War Lovers 'R Us?" I looked over at Chloe. I can't believe I had missed it. Her pink t-shirt read *I Voted for the POW*.

The two women didn't say another word to each other. I smiled and gave a friendly nod to Chloe's mom. She returned the grin. We didn't need to say anything to convey our unfortunate lack of surprise at what had just transpired. Soon enough, I was on my way to grab a quick snack at Whole Foods, then home to catch up on some news.

It's around 10:00 p.m. now. I'm still thinking about poor Oreo's face as he was yanked from his newfound buddy. If his owner couldn't stand the idea of her dog playing with a pup of a different political persuasion—well, you know what I mean—then I can only assume that her life is filled with people who are carbon copies of each other. I doubt she'd have enough tolerance (you know, that virtue the Left has claimed as its own) to endure someone like me for more than a millisecond.

What a small mind it must take to be comfortable walking day after day in those shoes.

* * * * *

"You know I love you, girl. But you're like an alien or something," an acquaintance from my acting days said to me as we inhaled pasta at an Italian eatery on 2nd Avenue.

"Wow, an alien. That's a first," I replied.

"How did you vote for that old geezer after he picked that hick from Alaska?"

"*Because* he picked that 'hick' from Alaska," I responded.

"But why? Why would you *ever* vote for her?" She looked troubled. Almost as much as that loon from the dog park the other day.

"Well, let's see. She has successfully run a business, a city, and a state. She'll take on her own party in a flash—and has—if it means getting a job done right. She isn't about to ditch her values to be popular with the media or with you and me. She understands the free market from being a part of it with her business, not from sitting in some stuffy library reading about it. And she doesn't seem to have an elitist bone in her body." She squinted at me, but didn't say a word. "And Obama? Why did you pull the lever for him?" I asked.

"Change and hope. We need both."

"What kind of change does he represent to you?" I asked. She began to fidget with her napkin.

"Just different things, you know. He's not your regular politician. He wants to change the whole country and the way things get done."

"How? How does he want to do that?" I asked.

"You know, just top to bottom, bottom to top."

"Like?"

"Just everything," she said in a raised voice. "Plus, he was a senator."

"What do you think of his voting record?" I asked.

"It was good."

"Do you agree with how he voted on issues?"

"Sure, yeah," she said as she shrugged.

"How so?"

"I don't know, in general," she quickly replied. "He's going to change the country for the better and bring back hope." She had no idea what Barack Obama stood for. She had memorized all the campaign slogans, but the buck stopped there. She did, however, know the details of Palin's Katie Couric interview and was familiar with the rumor—which she still thought was true— that Palin had banned books.

Sure, the media had played its part. But she also hadn't bothered to fact-check them in the least. Personal responsibility

… where has that value gone? *Your* choices, *your* country, *your* future. I set the record straight on what I could, but it didn't matter. She wanted her slogans and media-fed hype kept intact. The truth had little value in that equation.

I left the restaurant soon after and decided I needed a long walk. It was a quiet night—well, quiet by Manhattan standards. I found myself fixated on a poster in a store window of members of our armed forces. I said a quick prayer for those who lost their lives fighting for my right to be standing right there, right then. I could never repay them. I promised I'd always put my best foot forward in the name of their sacrifice.

I arrived home to an email from the girl I had eaten dinner with hours prior. She felt like we were just too different to sit across from each other anymore. *I felt so violated by your political views*, she wrote. I laughed louder and harder than I had in some time. And then I felt sad.

She's a nice girl with plenty of acting talent. I hope she'll make it in the biz someday, but if she's that threatened by a little Palin truth, she'll be eaten up by Hollywood in no time. I hope she finds it within herself to discover the principles that really guide her on the inside, not the ones that the media or her friends think should guide her. Because once she does, no one's talk will have the power to "violate" anything. That's one thing I know for sure.

* * * * *

I spent my free period in the faculty room flipping through newspapers and correcting quizzes. Two teachers nearby were chatting it up:

"My friend's daughter is dating a conservative at college and her family is going nuts."

"I don't blame them!"

"They're this really great Washington family that donated to Obama. And the daughter's boyfriend is this *Republican*."

"Well, maybe it's just a phase."

"That's what I told them. And what they're hoping for."

"What school are they at?"

"Brown."

"There are Republicans at Brown?"

"Not too many, but a few, I guess. It's like a disease that thankfully hasn't spread."

"Well, don't worry. It's curable."

I exited and was off to class. By mid-afternoon, I was feeling more tired than usual. I wish I could say that it was from teaching several periods of Spanish or from managing tricky

Dean matters, but no such luck. I was weary from the oodles of political comments that flooded me throughout the day. Several of my students were still stuck on the fact that I had raised my hand for McCain in the Election Day assembly. They felt the need to "remind" me that Obama is a "genius," Palin is an "idiot," and anything and everything is George W. Bush's fault.

"You know, the Constitution needs to get with the times, Ms. Bila. It's not the 1700s anymore," said a student as he crossed his arms.

"Yeah, Ms. B., and America needs to stop being so imperialistic," said another. I wondered what adult he had so adeptly quoted that from.

It went on and on. They wanted to know if I was a "war-lover" and why I "wear that American flag pin that sometimes doesn't match your outfit too well." I ignored 99.9% of it and shifted the focus back to verb conjugations. They were right about one thing, though. My pin sometimes doesn't match my outfit. But it always reminds me that no matter what life hands me on any particular day, I'm in the best place in the world to turn my lemons into lemonade.

Two classes were followed by a Palin-bashing session in the faculty room, during which I left and ate a snack on the bench outside. A group of students in the hallway were joking about how Republicans are dangerous because they don't believe in global warming. I waited briefly by the elevator, then deemed it best to opt for the stairs.

At 3:15, I hurried home and hit the gym for some much-needed refueling. I kept repeating to myself over and over, *You are a teacher and a Dean, just ignore the rest.* But playing blind and deaf just isn't my forte.

* * * * *

"You're a disgrace to women," one girl said to another at the table beside me. I had stopped at a coffee shop downtown to grab a green tea and chill out for a bit after school.

"It's just how I see it, that's all," the other replied. They couldn't have been more than seventeen.

"Well, you see it wrong, Lisa. Don't you care about women's rights? I mean, what are you, some kind of woman-hater?"

"No, I just believe what I believe. How am I a woman-hater because I don't believe in abortion?" Lisa asked.

"Lisa, do you realize that you're degrading us? Feminists have fought their whole lives for the pro-choice movement." *Ummm ... sure*, I thought. *Except for the mother of feminism and a bunch of the suffragists, but who's counting, right?*

"I'm sorry, but it just doesn't sit right with me. Those babies could grow up to be women too, right?" Lisa asked.

"It's not a baby at that point, Lisa. It's just tissue." *Aaah*, I thought. *The product of a Planned Parenthood education?*

Several more girls soon joined in. In no time at all, Lisa, the solitary pro-lifer, was under full-blown attack.

"Lisa, what's next? Should women stay at home and cook?"

"Well, only if they want to," Lisa replied shyly.

"Lisa, don't you see what an idiot you sound like? Do you want your rights trampled on?"

"Well, no, I mean—"

"—Then start acting like a woman, for God's sake."

"Yeah, Lisa, you're in New York now. Get with the program." *An out-of-towner,* I thought. *Interesting.*

"I don't know. I just feel what I feel. But maybe you're right," Lisa said. I looked over at her and stood up.

"Excuse me," I said to Lisa. "I don't mean to intrude, but I just want to say that you're one very inspiring young lady. I really appreciate what you had to say."

"Thank you," she replied as her face brightened. The rest didn't say a word. I smiled and hurried along.

There was something about giving that young woman the thumbs up that made me feel better than I had in a long time. I don't know for sure that it will make a difference in the long run. I don't know if she'll stick by her principles in the face of pressure to fit in with what's cool in Manhattan. But I know that something lit up inside her when she knew that a random stranger had been moved by her words. I hope she'll always remember that the greatest gift you can give yourself is to be proud of who you are, whether your biggest fans or most vocal opponents happen to like what you say.

I'm home now, flipping through images from an animal shelter of some of God's most beautiful creations. They'll always make me smile the biggest smiles and wish I could help them more than my wallet can spare. One day, I hope.

* * * * *

"What's a pretty young woman like you doing here all by yourself?" a thirty-something man with nerdy glasses and a suave demeanor said to me as I awaited the arrival of a friend at a bar on Bleecker Street.

"Waiting for a friend," I replied. I'll admit that the glasses did grab my attention for a second or two as he approached, but I was quickly soured by his over-the-top stride. Plus, I was distracted by a conversation going on nearby between a woman and a man about why "the French seem so much classier than your average hillbilly American." I could hear her saying, "You know, the ones outside of New York who wear those plaid shirts." I made a quick mental note to wear my flannel button-downs more often.

"Can I get you something to drink?" he asked. "I'm John."

"Oh, no thank you," I answered kindly. I lifted my bottle of water, and just as I did, he rushed to retrieve it.

"Let me get that for you," he said as he began working on the twist-off cap. After a couple of seconds of his unsuccessful turns, he asked the bartender for a bottle opener. I lifted the bottle, opened it, and took my first sip. "Well, what do we have here?" he asked. "A chick with a strong hand?" He raised his eyebrows and laughed. He had amused himself significantly.

"I guess you could say that," I answered. After about ten minutes of listening to him ramble on about his dad's business, his "luxury townhouse" in Soho, his former girlfriend's "ordinary family," and his upcoming "vacation of a lifetime" (I was mentally organizing my grocery list and wondering why his teeth had been whitened to a glow-in-the-dark shade), he delivered his proudest line: "You know, I worked on the Obama campaign." He was aglow.

I gave him a little nod as if to say *And?* He looked confused and repeated, "I worked on the Obama campaign." After a few seconds of silence, he added, "Did you hear me?"

I leaned in a bit. "I did, John. Let me say that you did an A+ job." He perked up pretty quickly. I continued: "Getting someone with that little experience and those disturbing associations elected is no small task. Tell me, did you coin the hope and change anthem?"

"There you are!" my friend said as she grabbed my arm. "Where have you been?"

"I've been right here, sipping this tasty water and hearing about how this perfect gentleman helped our good friend Obama get elected," I replied.

"Oh boy," she said. "Come on, let's go before you start talking fiscal this and ethical that."

"Well, John, it's been a pleasure," I said as I winked, took a final sip, and headed off to stuff my face.

I just got home and it's almost midnight. We had a lot of laughs. I drank one glass of wine and enjoyed a ride on the tipsy mobile. I know, I'm a big nerd. Every now and then John's deflated expression at my lack of fascination with his money and/or political contributions would enter my mind and I'd chuckle. Sorry to say that I don't have much patience for arrogance or stuck-up elitists. But the guy in the corner of the room who's too shy to come say hello, but flashes a nervous grin when I notice him—he's always had my interest.

The clock just struck twelve and it's Thanksgiving. Thank you, God, for my family, my friends, and my country. And for those flannel shirts that drive the highbrows wild.

* * * * *

"I just don't get you. What part of corruption plus racism equals Republican do you not understand?" my friend's roommate asked me at Starbucks this afternoon.

"Corruption and racism have nothing to do with Republican or Democrat," I answered.

"Yeah, right. Republicans are all for the big corporate boys. They get us into wars we don't want, tax the hell out of the poor, and couldn't care less about minorities."

"You *really* need to stop watching Keith Olbermann. Seriously, it's time for an intervention," I said. That led to ten minutes of him and his two friends shouting at me for "hating gay people" and being "a rich white girl." Fun fact: They were about three shades lighter—and three times more "rich"—than me.

I nibbled on my fruit salad and smiled as I thought about my sixty-six-year-old father who still works to pay his mortgage, and about how much my colorful friends would get a kick out of the anti-gay label my coffee "buddies" had cooked up for me. I was startled by a voice at the other end of the table.

"Guys! Leave her alone, for God's sake!" a young man shouted. He was super tall with a jet black mohawk. How had I missed him?

"Chill out," one of the other guys answered.

"No, *you* chill out! The girl has a different opinion. So what? Grow up, already," said the man with a mohawk. Silence quickly fell over the table. Within a few minutes, we were all on our way. I stopped the young man outside who had rushed to my defense.

"Thanks," I said.

"No need to thank me. Nice to meet you, though. I'm Chris, lefty liberal from Wyoming who loves that you have your own opinion."

"Nice to meet you, Chris," I said as I shook his hand. "I'm Jedediah, Reagan conservative from Manhattan who loves your mohawk." We both laughed and parted ways a few minutes later.

I spent my time at the gym thinking about my encounter this afternoon, about the amount of hair gel Chris must go through in a week, and about how cool it had been to have a stranger in Manhattan with a totally different opinion stand up for my right to disagree. That's what Manhattan needs more of—people, regardless of their views, fighting for everyone's right to see things differently. I also came to the very quick conclusion that I could never—ever—pull off a mohawk.

It's getting late and I likely won't be up much longer. Time to quickly catch up on some news and find out how many more members of the former Clinton staff will be adorning our soon-to-be president's era of hope and change.

December 2008

* * * * *

"I officially started my Bush countdown today," a teacher said this morning as she entered the faculty room.

"Me too!" said another.

"Me three!" said a third.

"I just can't believe that guy was ever elected," another added as I headed to class. I reentered the faculty room a few hours later, caught the first couple of sentences of an anti-Palin spiel, and opted for a seat on the hallway bench. I had plenty of grading to keep me busy.

Tonight I saw a guy on the subway wearing a t-shirt that read "I Support the NRA." He was about 6'5" and well over two-hundred pounds of muscle. People stared, but no one said a peep. One young man wearing a Columbia University sweatshirt rolled his eyes and sighed pretty conspicuously.

"You got a problem?" asked the man in the NRA shirt.

"Oh no, no problem," said the ivy-leaguer as he slid down in his seat. *Cat got your tongue?* I thought. I'll never understand people who are opposed to everyday citizens protecting themselves. Constitution aside, what is it about a world in which only the police and criminals carry guns that they find so enchanting?

Tonight I sampled a different spin class. It started out pretty well. In fact, I was pleasantly surprised to hear the instructor begin by telling us she had no time for sissies. I couldn't have said it better myself. But roughly ten minutes later, she said this: "Come on, people. Push your bodies. Your bodies need change. Bring your bodies some Obama-style change." *Good grief* was my first thought. My second was, *Wait, so you want me to work out for an hour, then redistribute my muscle tone to someone else?*

I stopped by a deli soon after to pick up lentils, salsa, and bottled water. Oh, and those fruit snacks that look like ruler-sized fruit roll-ups. I fell in love with a Pomeranian named Boxer dressed in a badass army jacket. His mom told me that her husband is in the army and that Boxer wears army gear every day in honor of him.

Boxer stood tall—all ten pounds of him. He followed all commands and guarded his mom like a trooper. His dad would be proud. I took a photo of him with my phone and stared at it for the next half-hour.

I'm off to call my mom to tell her how much I miss Bronte. Bronte's the family cat who lives with my parents. She's a little mean and tough as nails, with a fierce independent streak. I love her to death ... even when she hisses at me for disturbing her in the sixth hour of a seven-hour nap. She'd look smokin' hot in an army jacket.

Good night, all. Sleep tight. Don't let Bill Clinton bite.

* * * * *

I went to FAO Schwarz after work today. Yes, I bought the enormous brown teddy bear. No, I won't sleep with it at night. Well … not *every* night.

While perusing the electronics section—my gosh, they sell all but a terminator these days—I overheard a conversation between two boys, each around twelve years old.

"Ben, if you want the game, you're gonna have to save up for it."

"Why?" Ben asked. "I'll just talk my mom into getting it for me. If I tell her I'll pay her back, she'll buy it."

"Well, are you gonna pay her back?"

"No. She doesn't need the money. Have you seen my house?" Ben asked.

"Yeah, but still, Ben. You get an allowance. If you say you're gonna pay her back, you should pay her back."

"Whatever, Tim. By the time she asks me for it, I'll have spent my allowance. Then she'll yell at me for like two seconds and give me more." Tim nodded in disapproval. "What's your problem? How you gonna pay for yours?"

"I saved up," Tim said.

"Sucks to be you," Ben replied.

"It's not so bad. I feel grown up, you know?"

"No way. I'm staying a kid for as long as I can to get stuff for free. Come on, let's get pizza. It's on my mom," Ben said as he waved a ten-dollar bill in the air and smirked. Tim rolled his eyes and followed him out.

I stood in the aisle for a few minutes looking at the exit door. I had been intrigued by their conversation and now I knew why. Tim and Ben had perfectly expressed—without likely having much comprehension of the political world—two ideologies that couldn't have been more different.

Think about it. Tim, the practical saver who had been raised to value hard-earned cash. Frankly, he had a greater sense of fiscal responsibility than most U.S. senators. Ben, the big spender who felt it was his mother's job to accommodate his every desire. I mean, he was *entitled* to those toys, right? It was fascinating to witness such a striking difference between the thought processes of two kids. I wonder what their future voting tendencies will be.

I'm off to bed soon, right after I check out some puppy adoption photos and call to say good night to my number one girl, Bronte. My mom says she hissed at a friend of hers who had a pro-Obama outburst at our house.

Yep, Bronte's *definitely* a Bila.

* * * * *

A "friend" called me this afternoon. The conversation went like this:

"I'm sorry I haven't been in touch," she said. "Do you know why?"

"No, I just figured you felt offended by my Facebook status updates again," I answered.

"Oh no, I don't read them," she replied. "I hope this doesn't upset you, but I really try not to."

"It doesn't upset me, but can I ask why you don't?"

"Because I just know that what you're saying is wrong. I don't know why, but I just know it is. Just the word conservative alone—"

"—What about it?" I interjected.

"I don't even know. I just know that I was brought up to know that conservatives aren't good people. And people I've met … conservative people … always just rub me the wrong way."

"As in how?" I asked.

"Just their view of the rest of the world and the poor. I know liberals can be a little too bleeding-heart and care too much about the poor, but conservatives don't care at all. They're just not my kind of people."

"Why do you think conservatives don't care about the poor and liberals do? Where did you get that from?" I asked.

"I don't know. That's just what I've always been taught," she said. "And when I meet conservatives, they're always like, 'America this' or 'America that.' Anyway, I don't want to talk about it."

"But we should," I replied. "Those things you said—"

"—No, I don't want to talk about it," she interjected.

"But—"

"—No!"

She was horrified by the idea of hearing another viewpoint. She didn't know why she disliked the people she was supposed to dislike, and she didn't want to find out that maybe she shouldn't be disliking them at all. Perhaps she was afraid of—heaven forbid—finding herself in agreement with one of my Facebook posts.

I ended the conversation quickly, as I didn't have much left to say. I knew that I could never be close to someone who made the choice to walk through life with blinders on. I'll never understand security in ignorance. It wouldn't bother me in the least if she disagreed with me, but her insistence on doing so without knowing why was something else entirely. As was the fact that she never did take the time to ask me what I actually believe. She preferred a strict devotion to what *The New York Times* told her I stand for.

I'm off to Whole Foods for some much-needed guacamole and chips. You know, right after I "America this" and "America that." God bless America. LOVE IT OR LEAVE IT.

* * * * *

I woke up this morning thinking about my college valedictory speech for some reason. It marked one of the most special days in my life. And it had nothing to do with the fact that I was the valedictorian.

I remember standing up there on stage, quoting some combination of Marcel Proust and my favorite Spanish author, Soledad Puértolas, looking out at a big crowd. My eyes zeroed in on my two best friends many rows apart from each other, both making funny faces and bizarre gestures to try to make me laugh. I remember thinking that never again in my life would I meet two people so dramatically different from me—and from each other—whom I would love so much.

We were our own version of "The Three Stooges" back then, and walking down the street on any given day we surely looked like people you'd never in a million years expect to be standing side-by-side. Everything from our clothing to our personalities to our hobbies couldn't have been more different. And that's what made us great. I've never lost that sentiment—that appreciation for the differences in people—or the knowledge that individuality is a beautiful thing.

While at school today, I sat in the faculty room and tried to ignore an animated conversation about why Canadians would ever want to come to the United States when "they have such a beautiful, harmonious country, unlike us." It soon gave way to their hopeful declarations that Texas would one day secede and that Americans "would learn to acquire more European-style sophistication." I gathered my books and returned to my newfound home, the hallway bench.

While I was walking home around 3:00 p.m., I saw two women wearing "Fight Obesity" t-shirts. They were seated in one of those bicycle carts being driven around by a young, slender gentleman.

At a diner, I overheard a discussion among four college students about why the government should tax fast food so that kids would be discouraged from eating it. They were all in agreement. And yet it never occurred to a single one of them to take some initiative and put down the burgers and fries.

I headed to the gym around 7:00, clad in my "Texas Rodeo" t-shirt in honor of my work colleagues, then hurried to call my friend Lauren to plan a ski trip we'd likely never find time to put on the map.

Oh, and I've decided on a female Maltese, mostly because it's one of the few breeds that don't make me sneeze. She'll be a

71

tomboy (like her mom), will have a full conservative wardrobe, and will melt my heart in a quarter of a second.

Only one week left until Christmas break. Lone Star tree ornaments for the teachers at school? Tempting. Very tempting.

* * * * *

Two women were arguing in the elevator of my building this morning about who is cuter, Barack Obama or Bill Clinton. They went on to reluctantly admit that Sarah Palin is a bit of a looker, but quickly followed it up with how she'd never in a million years survive in Midtown Manhattan. Right, ladies. The woman hunts eight-hundred pound moose, runs God-knows-how-many miles a day, nets hundreds of salmon in a boat the size of your bathrooms, and thinks nothing of ten-degree weather. But you're right. How would she ever have the endurance for a five-minute wait for a taxi outside of Bloomingdales or a ten-minute subway ride to Union Square? I couldn't help but laugh, the image of either of those ladies shoveling snow in Wasilla or dressed in garb adorned with fish guts too entertaining for words.

I spent some time in a library this afternoon, the perfect shelter from a cold day, the scent of old books exactly what I needed. I sifted through unknown texts like I often do in antique bookstores, and was able to lose myself in the lives of strangers. I was occasionally jolted out of my imaginary world by the conversations of those around me.

Two girls were organizing a meeting of a socialist club to bring about awareness of "the dangers of capitalism" and how it "keeps people down." One was carrying a Louis Vuitton handbag and the other soon shifted the discussion to plans of a spring break cruise to the Caribbean. That darn capitalism. Keepin' the folks down left and right.

An hour or so later, I overheard two professors whispering about how 9/11 had quite possibly been orchestrated by President Bush so that he could brand himself as a hero. I couldn't begin to imagine what their lesson plans looked like.

As I enjoyed a quick snack outside, a bunch of students were discussing an Obama inauguration party. They couldn't stop gushing about what a "cool" president he would be and how the rest of the world "would finally like us." I wondered if they had thought about the fact that the rest of the world likes us plenty when we're protecting their freedoms, aiding their poor, and/or supporting their battles against tyrants.

I made a brave attempt at an outdoor run this evening and quickly found out that I'm not as tough as I thought. I'm not sure I was dressed quite right, as I couldn't feel my legs for the better part of the twenty minutes I lasted. I suddenly had a newfound respect for Sarah Palin. I also wished I could give her a call and ask her where she buys her insulated gear. Regardless, I made a vow to run outside in the cold at least once per winter month. There's nothing like discovering something that makes you realize you have some work to do in the tough department. Bring it on, January. I'll be waiting. With layers. And a ski mask. And *lots* of lip balm.

While I was walking home from the deli tonight, I spotted a little girl who was lost. She was about six years old and surprisingly calm. I stood with her for a few minutes, asking some questions I hoped would help me to get her back home. Her mom soon darted out of a nearby store in a panic, tears streaming down her cheeks, and embraced her daughter. She thanked me and I could tell that she loved that child with everything she had.

"What's your name?" the little girl asked me.

"Jedediah," I replied. "I know, it's a tough one. And yours?"

"Emma," she answered. She grinned and looked up at me with the most adorable, bashful eyes. "I like your button," she said as she pointed up. "It's America. I love America." I smiled. I was wearing a black fleece, and on the collar was an American flag pin.

"Thank you, Emma," I replied. She soon skipped off with her mom.

I'm off to bed, but I'm still thinking about that little girl. There was something special about her, something very adult for such a tiny person. Someone in her house certainly did something right. She may not have understood the depths of what my button meant, but she knew that it stood for America. And that it represents something darn good.

* * * * *

Today we had early dismissal at school because it's the first day of our holiday recess. We walked over to a nearby congregation this morning, as we always do on the last day of school before break. Students filed in and we watched the school choir sing an assortment of Jewish and Christian songs. The caroling is always lovely, and seeing the lower school students perform warms my heart. Their smiles and excitement are definitely some of life's greatest gifts.

Right before the singing began, a high school student had this exchange with an adult:

"I don't like churches," the student said. "They give me the creeps."

"Well, this one's very secular, so you don't have to worry about it," the adult answered.

"But isn't it Christian?" the girl asked.

"Well, it has Christian roots, but it's different. Don't worry, it's tolerant-Christian," the adult replied. Just as I looked up at him, the ceremony began.

Tolerant-Christian. Wow. I was disgusted. I don't know what I would've said if the ceremony hadn't begun at that moment.

The festivities ended pretty quickly and I was one of the first out the door. I couldn't get the image of that adult out of my mind, of the way he had led that kid to believe that whatever fear of churches she had acquired along the way was justified, and that the words Christian and tolerant were typically incompatible.

The rest of the day was particularly uneventful. I spent some time watching old movies, attempted to cook dinner, and took a bundled walk in the cold that felt wonderful. Around 10:00 p.m., I lit a couple of candles by my bedside—that's the little church I've come to call my own—and asked God to light the path I was meant to follow. And to help me to handle everything that was sure to come with it.

* * * * *

Greetings from Fort Myers, Florida! My parents and I decided to seize the opportunity for some family time this week, so we headed down to a place we know all too well. We lived here for a few years when I was just a tiny tot. My dad managed a hotel on the Gulf and I attended kindergarten at a local private school. It was one of the few times that so many of the people I loved most were in the same place—mom and dad, my two closest aunts, a cousin, and even one set of grandparents for a bit. I'll never forget building snowmen out of sand for Christmas, a *Snow White and the Seven Dwarfs* beach party for my fourth birthday, and waking up every morning to the sound of the ocean. I was so small, so wide-eyed, but somehow there was always a part of me that was a little more grown up than it should have been.

I remember that when my parents enrolled me in the first grade in Staten Island, one of the first school projects I was assigned was to tell a story about what I had learned over the past few months. Lots of kids talked about how their moms or dads had taught them how to ride a bike, how cousins had shown them how to hit a baseball, or how they had managed to swim without water wings. Mine was a little different. I talked about how if you look long and hard enough at a sunset or a great big ocean, you'll realize that there's something way bigger than you out there ... and much, much stronger. I remember that my first-grade teacher called home that afternoon to ask if my mother had told me what to say. She hadn't. Mom had laughed and told my teacher that sometimes my flair for the dramatic gets the better of me. I had no idea what that meant.

Anyway, here we are again, right on the Gulf of Mexico. The sand still feels like home.

We went to a local Publix today to pick up some groceries. While I was sifting through my bag for money to pay for two boxes of oranges and some ingredients for homemade burritos, a woman tapped me on the shoulder.

"You dropped this," she said with a smile, holding out my "Palin Power" pin, which had fallen out of my purse.

"Oh, thanks," I answered.

"I'm a lifelong Democrat. I didn't vote for her, but kudos to you for speaking your mind," she said. "Love to see young people involved."

"Thanks," I replied. I went on to pay, then headed to the car and back to the condo we're renting.

Something felt so bizarre about the encounter I'd just had. There she was, a Democrat who didn't vote for Palin, picking up my pin and giving me a pat on the back for my very different opinion? And then it hit me. Whatever is floating around in the air down here needs to be bottled, packaged, and delivered to Manhattan A.S.A.P.

January 2009

* * * * *

I went to a New Year's Eve party in the East Village last night with an acquaintance. She kept introducing me as her "conservative friend from college." One of the men asked me if I thought President Bush "has a learning disability." His friend wanted to know how rich my parents are. About an hour later, another asked me if I'm "a religious freak."

I spent a good part of the evening dancing my butt off and mingling. Of course, I was told on numerous occasions that I don't *look* like a conservative or *dance* like a conservative. They couldn't understand why I knew all the lyrics to Madonna's eighties hits and wasn't sporting a string of pearls around my neck and a tailored suit.

I was entirely amused by what they thought your standard, pre-packaged conservative should do, wear, and say. It's incredible how a mind prone to collectivism will quickly try to impose that same branding on you. I hate to break it to them, but individuality is still alive and well in this country.

I finished off the evening spinning around to the sound of Cyndi Lauper and sipping the remains of my first and only glass of white wine. Yes, I was tipsy. Yes, I'm lame. Haven't we been through this already?

This morning, I hit the gym for some much-needed running. It was quite a comical scene, as I was wearing my Founding Fathers tank and was right smack in the middle of a young gentleman sporting a MoveOn.org t-shirt and an older lady wearing a pro-Obama hoodie. Like any typical day in Manhattan, I was outnumbered. But hey, I had the guys who won the American Revolution on my side.

Just before diving into some macaroni tonight, I received an email from an acquaintance who had been engaging in political debates with me for a month or so. She's a self-professed socialist. We had gone back and forth three or four times on policy issues and I appreciated her passion for the art of debate. She had generally been respectful in her disagreement, and I valued the mostly civil exchanges we had shared ... until today's email, that is.

I sort of knew something had snapped when she began with, "You really are a right-wing immigrant-hater." She went on to include such glowing descriptions as "protector of the rich" and "warmonger," among other gracious selections. The cause?

Something about my tribute to my great-grandparents, immigrants from Italy who busted their butts to come to America to build a life for themselves, didn't sit right with her. My admiration for legal immigration to the United States, and rejection of the illegal alternative, somehow made me the enemy. She closed by saying that I deserved to "feel the pain of those illegal immigrants." I responded by asking where I could sign up for the liberal compassion courses that had taught her so much.

I'm headed to bed now. Just one quick call to mom and dad, and a peek at some mindless television to lull me to sleep. I hope that 2009 brings lots of laughs, a clean bill of health, pleasant surprises, and newfound inspiration. Oh, and a puppy I will spoil with everything I have.

* * * * *

I can't wrap my head around how many times I've been called a racist because I'm not an Obama supporter. It really has become the involuntary response of liberals to anyone who opposes his far-left voting record. It's as if no one could possibly disagree with his vision for America based on what he has said and done. Nope, must be the color of his skin. Do they actually believe that crap, or do they just have nothing better to say?

Of course, it's all a bunch of bull. A quick glance at my friendships and dating history will reveal a medley of people of all shapes, sizes, colors, and backgrounds. The truth is that I don't give a rat's tush whether Barack Obama is white, black, green, or tie-dyed. But that doesn't matter one bit to the loons who would rather protect their faulty comeback than ponder an ounce of truth. Now on to the day's highlights ...

On my way home from a friend's apartment, I witnessed two taxi drivers nearly kill each other in Soho. A group of men dressed in drag (who had hair and makeup to die for) walked up Sixth Avenue. A string of "For Sale" signs in store windows featured items at a mere 30% above sensible pricing. And a band of guys played some pretty awesome music by Union Square Park. It was a typical Manhattan afternoon.

I slipped on the remains of someone's fruit smoothie on the corner of my block and plunged head first into a guy selling discounted scarves and hats. I knocked over a small stack of Obama "Hope" pins. It was an accident, but a funny one. He was incredibly kind. I apologized for being a klutz and headed home, but was briefly distracted by the sound of salsa music coming from somewhere nearby. There's just something about that sound I can't resist. But that's a *whole* other story.

I arrived home to a handwritten letter—my absolute favorite—from a friend. She was just saying hello, hoping that all is well in my world, and inviting me on a vacation to San Francisco. I wrote her back on my favorite stationery, purchased from an antique book shop. It looks like it has been through hell and back, which is why I adore it. I told her I'd love to go, but only if I could bring as much pro-U.S. military garb as I could gather and a copy of the Constitution for Pelosi. There's a small chance she may disinvite me.

I'm suddenly reminded of that guy who asked me out on several occasions, but stopped me on the street last week to tell me he needed to retract his invites because he saw me wearing a shirt with a conservative slogan. After having said no to him about six times, you can imagine that it was a tough pill for me to swallow. I'll try to pick up the pieces and carry on.

I'm off to listen to some sappy music and sort through online puppy photos, while catching up on news and attempting to cook something edible. Something with pumpernickel bread. I never could get into white bread.

I know, I know. I'm a racist.

* * * * *

I witnessed a hilarious fight while waiting for a friend on Fifth Avenue this afternoon. Two women—both self-proclaimed feminists—were engaged in a feisty debate over whether Sarah Palin is anti-feminist or anti-woman.

One of the women insisted that she's anti-feminist because she's pro-life. The other refused to concede, affirming that she's anti-woman because she "hunts like a man, fishes like a man, and tries to talk tough like a man." Ummm, what was that about feminism again?

They ultimately met somewhere in the middle, defining her as "a disgrace to women." I found it quite entertaining, as are most heated exchanges with plenty of histrionics and no facts. The funniest part of it all was that the women actually felt like they were disagreeing, like they were attacking an argument from completely opposing sides of the aisle. Manhattan-style political diversity. Gotta love it.

I was approached by a guy in my building's elevator this evening. He wanted to know what business I thought I had wearing my "Keep the Change" sweatshirt around the neighborhood. When I responded by telling him I'd gladly stick a copy of the First Amendment in his mailbox, he became frenzied and began shouting about how George W. Bush is a "domestic terrorist." He scared the hell out of a miniature poodle in the lobby.

An acquaintance met me for dinner around 8:00. While on our way to a vegan restaurant, he informed me that he would have to delete me as a Facebook friend because my posts are "just too right-wing." He felt "hurt" and "wronged" by my links to such "hateful" sources as *Human Events* and The Heritage Foundation. I made a brief attempt at asking why he had taken my news links so personally, but he was too "distressed" to talk about it. Needless to say, the rest of the dinner didn't go so well. Let's just say you could hear the crickets chirping.

When I arrived home, I signed on to Facebook to remove him as he had requested. I took a quick glance at his page before deleting him. I noticed that he had recently joined a Bush-bashing group. I also saw that I had an email from him from hours prior, in which he had called me a "brainwashed idiot." That somehow didn't meet his definition of "hateful."

I felt like writing him back. However, I quickly reminded myself that there's no talking to perpetual victims who fire their figurative rifles, but run to the corner and sob when someone answers back. There's no reasoning with someone who can't read news links without feeling personally offended.

I've had enough of the hypocrisy, political correctness, and cry-baby syndrome of some on the left as they call you whatever, whenever, however without blinking an eye. That includes any and all who feel persecuted by my right to an opinion.

* * * * *

The faculty room was filled today with all the hustle and bustle of the days before Christmas. After all, it's just one week until the arrival of "hope" and "change." Many teachers were giddy with anticipation, adorned with ear-to-ear smiles and chanting the likes of "It's almost here!" and, my personal favorite, inspired by Mrs. Obama herself: "For the first time in my adult life, I'm proud of my country!" I spent most of my free periods—you guessed it—on the hallway bench.

Quite a few kids could hardly contain themselves as well. I heard at least two "He's going to be the best president we've ever had," one "Yes we can," and more than a handful of "I can't wait to have a cool president."

After school, I had agreed to help the son of a friend with some homework. Spanish doesn't come easily to him, and we spent over an hour working on drills of verb conjugations. He's a diligent high school student and wasn't going to put the books down until he knew he had at least a B+ in the bag. When he finally felt comfortable and we had wrapped things up, he asked me to read over a short essay he'd written on why Barack Obama will make a great president. I was soon horrified to see wealth redistribution glorified as a founding American principle.

We talked about it for a bit, and he simply couldn't understand why I'm opposed to the idea. Much like a student I had helped out a short time ago, he was quick to remind me that I'm on the poor end of the spectrum and would benefit quite a bit. Charming, I know. I thought about what he had said for a few moments, and then I replied:

"You know what? I've been thinking about all the studying you put into Spanish and what a hard worker you are. And that's pretty awesome for a young kid. But let's face it—some kids just don't have that kind of commitment. What if there's too much noise in their houses while they're trying to study? Or they can't call forth the diligence? Or they're just plain busy with other stuff? Who knows? But seeing as though you don't really *need* an A+, why don't we make a deal? If you get above a 90%, you toss some points over to them."

He was outraged. "What? Have you lost your mind? I've been working my ass off all week and now you want me to hand points over to my friends, who have been partying or not studying or whatever?"

"Well, why not?" I asked.

"Because it's stupid. That's like telling them it's okay not to study and telling me that the harder I work, the more punished I'll get. Plus, why should they have a right to my points?"

"Exactly," I said. "And that, my friend, is why I oppose redistribution of wealth." I smiled, stood up, and was on my way. He sat quietly, staring into space as I exited.

I don't know that my analogy will make a big difference to him as he grows up and experiences more of the world, but I know that it made him think. And if I was able to get that very bright young man to step outside the box he has been programmed to see the world through for just a second, then I consider it a good day's work.

* * * * *

I counted nine kids wearing t-shirts with images of Barack Obama at school today, some with the MoveOn.org logo. I saw three teachers give them a thumbs up with big smiles. One of the teachers also gave me a weird look when she noticed my American flag pin.

I went to JFK Airport tonight to pick up a friend. Her flight was delayed. As I nibbled on a muffin and alternated between sitting and roaming, I heard some interesting conversations.

Two twenty-somethings from Spain were talking about how women in America have managed to earn a kind of workplace respect they don't feel they have in their country. They vowed to save their money and move to New York City, which they called "the capital of the world." An older British gentleman was telling his wife about plans to revisit the U.S. for an appointment regarding the surgery he'd just had in Manhattan. And a Canadian woman was talking with a business partner about the death of free speech in Canada. I thought about all the stories my liberal friends treasure about how the rest of the world hates what America stands for. It brought some much-needed amusement to my otherwise tedious wait.

After a great dinner and lots of laughs, I received a call from my grandmother. She's ninety-four and just about as feisty as you could imagine. If you're wondering what I mean, let's take a look at some examples.

When my mom asked her what she wanted for her birthday this year, Nanny said she wanted to go bowling. And not just any bowling, but the cosmic kind—you know, where the lanes are traced in neon and you bowl in the dark.

Nanny went shopping with my mom last week. When a girl in the fitting room kept asking if she looked fat, Nanny stuck out her head and replied, "A little in the gut, honey." She has also been known to talk about sex, love, and rock and roll with greater ease than my mother would like. She never attended high school or college, but got her education from the streets of Brooklyn and from being the eldest of thirteen children. My grandfather was always quick to admit that she scared the crap out of him.

Anyway, Nanny phoned me tonight to chat about how a woman had made fun of her McCain pin in the bank, saying, "The election's over, grandma. You lost." Her response had been filled with some not-so-nice words and the statement, "Actually, America lost." She also wanted to share with me some words of wisdom: "You know, kid, you went to school all those years and studied like crazy, for what? Do something big. Do it because you can."

Maybe she's right. I'm going to have to think about that one for a bit. But I'll get back to you.

* * * * *

Well, it's Inauguration Day. I saw more Obama gear than I could count on my way to work. School was alive with a heightened energy, and many students were garnished with "Hope" and "Change" pins. The faculty room was stirring with an assortment of Bush jokes, most of which weren't funny and would have been labeled offensive had they been applied to Obama. Two females at a nearby bagel shop couldn't stop gushing about "how handsome Barack is," while a friend of theirs rejoiced in the end to what he called "America's reign of terror."

The inauguration was streamed live on a large screen in the auditorium and in a conference room. I caught as much of it as I could while working. I was also counting down the minutes until I could head home and hit the sack, as my neighbors had spent the hours from three to five a.m. engaged in yet another wrestling match. I was beat.

I knew that the inauguration had finished when I heard an administrator shout, "He's out! The moron is out!" As I headed to my classroom, I noticed a teacher exchanging high-fives with kids in the hallway. More Bush jokes followed ad nauseam.

George W. Bush and I share some policy differences for sure, but I give that man an abundance of credit. To be able to withstand perpetual, nonsensical attacks takes some serious character. My guess is that at the end of the day, his sense of what matters and what doesn't is strong enough to help him ignore most of the garbage that comes his way. I do wish he'd answer them back just once, though.

As I sat in the hallway finishing up some notes, one of the new teachers asked me why I wasn't excited. I replied by saying that I didn't know what I should be excited about.

"Obama!" he exclaimed. I didn't answer. "Did you not vote for him?" he asked with disbelief.

"I didn't," I replied. He rolled his eyes and walked away.

I left school around 3:30 and decided to run some errands. A bartender on Third Avenue was wearing an Obama party hat—you know, those triangle-shaped ones you see at kids' birthday parties. It was a sight I may never forget. I stopped by a friend's apartment around 6:00, but when the conversation shifted over to how Republicans should be "hung out to dry," I thought it best to leave.

It's been a long day and I'm off to write for a bit. I wish President Obama and his family a healthy transition, but I sure hope his policies look nothing like I think they will.

* * * * *

My friend and I headed upstate this afternoon. We had lunch at a small, old-fashioned café, walked around, and met up with his friends for dinner at a quaint restaurant. I love long drives, particularly in and out of small American towns where the owner of the corner store knows everyone by name, and families can sit around on the porch talking about that vacation last year when Uncle X and Aunt Y had too many margaritas and took a karaoke bar by storm. I know it sounds a little cliché, but I guess I've always wanted a taste of that life.

We passed countless gorgeous homes enriched by history's brushstroke, so many of them with American flags out front. The flags looked strong. There was something in their posture that mirrored the endurance of the country they represent. Or maybe it was all in my gaze, in the love I possess for America and the way those flags spoke to me as a result. I wish there were more of them on the streets of Manhattan.

My friend and I got into a fun political debate with his buddies, who referred to themselves as "hard-core Democrats." They're assertive guys who clearly love big government, but something very strange happened. They listened when I spoke, offered healthy debate, and asked my opinion on a number of issues. Where was the name-calling, the refusal to sit at my table because I harbor a different world view, the horror at the thought that people of my political ideology exist?

They were liberal, but they weren't elitists. And they hadn't lost touch with the tolerance they preached. I instantly thought of the woman in Fort Myers who had picked up my Palin pin from the floor and patted me on the back for getting involved. I've always felt that elitism—on the left and the right—is what's eating away at our country. The more walks I take through small American towns, the more I know that's true.

On the drive home, I caught a glimpse of the insides of some of those classic houses. The lights were on and I could see a little girl and her mom in one kitchen cooking something, a family watching TV in a living room, and a couple sitting before a fireplace. There was something about the stillness of the night, the quiet in the air, that seemed to make time slow down from the hectic comings and goings of Manhattan. I had a chance to think, to look, and to feel. I wished I could capture that stillness and bring it back home.

Manhattan was as busy as ever, and a fight between a couple outside my building and the honking of two angry taxi drivers brought a quickness back to my stride, an urgency to my thoughts, and the sentiment that I had way too much to do and far too little time. I hurriedly stopped off at a nearby restaurant to pick up some takeout, and while I was waiting, witnessed a conversation—or shall I say, a shouting match—between two women. They were disagreeing about the educational system in New York City. By the time my food had arrived, one had called the other a "stupid-assed nitwit" and she had replied, "You moron, go get an education from a real school and come talk to me."

Yep, I was home.

* * * * *

So, today is my birthday. People keep asking me how it feels to hit the big 3-0. The truth is that I've been sort of acting like I'm thirty since the age of ten, so the transition has been quite painless.

I really was a bizarre little creature right from the start. I never crawled. Mom says I used to pull myself up and hold onto things to get around. At eleven months old, I just stood up and walked across my grandmother's living room.

My first sentence was "Open the door." Mom had been busy putting away groceries, dad was knocking, and I was impatient— as always.

I decided at the age of three that I wanted to read. So I did. Once again, I didn't have much patience for the process, though. On my fourth birthday, my mom found me on the floor of her closet holding *The Great Gatsby*. She says I insisted on repeating the first few lines with her over and over again until I got them right.

I was also a bit of an oddball in that I didn't like being around kids. I'd become solemn when my mom would make me go to birthday parties, and I would beg to be dropped off at my nanny's house to hang out with her seventy-something friends instead. I've always felt strangely at home with people much older than me. Now that I think of it, not much has changed in the past thirty years.

Anyway, I decided to spend my big 3-0 watching my friend's little cousin play basketball. It wasn't an official game, but had been organized by some of the parents, and the kids were psyched. It was pretty intense for a bunch of ten-year-olds. They passed, leaped, and ran with more gusto than I often see in the NBA. The determination and commitment in their eyes made me proud, even though I had never met any of them.

About two minutes before the game ended, the dad of one of the boys jumped up and shouted, "Go get him, tiger! Show him who's boss!" His son was playing pretty impressive defense. In fact, that's what won his team the game.

As I stood by the exit door waiting for my friend to return from chatting with his family, a woman approached the coach and nastily asked to speak with him. Before he had a chance to say a word, she began a tirade about how the gentleman sitting beside me had incited violence, and how his son shouldn't be allowed to play in the future.

"What did he say?" the coach asked.

"He told *his* son to show *my* son who's boss! He yelled, 'Go get him, tiger!'" I was trying so hard to contain my laughter. So was the coach.

"Sorry, ma'am," he answered. "But that's typical game talk. I'm sure he wasn't trying to do any harm, so I wouldn't worry about it."

"Well, I *am* worried!" she exclaimed. She went on. And on. And on. And then her punch line: "If you're going to practice Dick Cheney-style tactics here, my son is out!" I burst out laughing and she turned to look at me with shock, grabbed her son by the arm, and stormed out. The coach and I spent the next five minutes wondering how in the heck her poor kid hasn't lost his mind living with a nutcase.

I spent the rest of the night having dinner and talking with my best friend. We reminisced about my twenty-fifth birthday— which we also spent together—and how I wouldn't stop conversing with that forty-something dude at the bar who looked like Robert Redford, but nerdier.

I'm headed to bed soon and I'm thinking about that ridiculous woman at the basketball game. I feel sorry for her son, who may never learn the importance of shrugging off what someone has to say about you and becoming that much stronger as a result. I hope he won't grow up to be too afraid to call it like he sees it.

My birthday wish for 2009: health, guidance toward where I'm meant to be, and—you guessed it—a Maltese!

February 2009

* * * * *

My friend came to visit from out of town today. She grew up in New York City, but moved south during high school because her dad's company transferred him there. She arrived around 3:00 this afternoon. I welcomed the chill-out time, as I had spent my morning dodging faculty discussions about how it's the duty of the federal government to bail out failing businesses and how Barack Obama is a post-racial president.

We had a wonderful lunch, caught up on some details of the past few months, and temporarily parted ways as she met up with an old friend. She returned to my apartment a few hours later and looked frazzled.

"What the hell is in the drinking water in this city?" she asked.

"Why? What's up?" I replied. She went on to disclose that she had met up with friends of her friend in Soho, and when the subject came up of where she was living, they unanimously suggested that she move to "a real city." They proceeded to refer to Texas as "a bunch of intolerants." When they found out that she isn't an Obama supporter, they called her "simple-minded" and insisted that she had been brainwashed.

On her way back to meet me, she got stopped by a woman handing out flyers for a pro-choice campus function. When she declined by saying that she is pro-life, the lady followed her for a quarter of a block, asking if she wanted to be responsible for "the death of the women's movement." She said nothing in response, as she doesn't have a sarcastic bone in her body. I wish I had been there to throw in a little, *So, is killing unborn female fetuses a prerequisite for sustaining the women's movement?*

We spent the night ordering in, watching an old movie, and talking about how her life has changed since she moved. She said that being back here did feel like coming home in a sense, but that she didn't think New York City was a place she'd ever want to live in again. She said that her stand on the issues can sometimes be a little out of place among her circle in Texas (she's a self-proclaimed "moderate Independent"), but that she had never felt like she was under attack for her opinions until today.

The whole conversation made me sad. When I look at Manhattan, I see one of the most beautiful places in the world. Some have critiqued it for being an "old city," but that's precisely why I love it. The richness of the buildings, the touch of old brownstones ... there's just nothing like it, no better way to remind yourself of all the people who have walked before you. What a shame that someone could visit such a gorgeous work of art, a supposed hub of diversity, and leave feeling like she just couldn't be herself in this space—not without being badgered for it.

New York City is capable of much bigger and better than that.

* * * * *

My friend called me this morning to tell me she's getting a divorce ... over politics. At first, I thought it was silly. Sure, she's a conservative and her husband is a liberal. But, so what? There must be dozens of other things they have in common that could make up for that, right? She replied with this: "It's almost impossible to share your life with someone who has a completely different view of the world than you do." She had an interesting point.

She and her husband have been married for a year. Once the shock of her divorce news wore off, I started to think about all the phone calls she and I have shared over the past twelve months. Maybe I shouldn't have been so surprised by their parting.

Just last week, they had a big fight over contraception. She doesn't want kids for a few years, and is hence particularly strict about birth control. His off-the-cuff comment about how she should loosen up because "This isn't 1900 and you could just get an abortion" didn't go over too well with her.

Thanksgiving dinner wasn't so pleasant for them, either. I remember her calling me that night to tell me that her husband had made fun of her father's gun collection and had asked her father why he felt the need to "masculinize" himself with weapons. Her father is a Marine. As I recall, the conversation ended with her father suggesting that her husband study the Second Amendment and "grow a pair."

Some time around Christmas, she and her husband got into a big argument. She was disgusted that a friend of hers who works in the public school system and is a darn good teacher is subject to the same incremental pay increases as everyone else. It led to a shouting match outside of Rockefeller Center, and I feared I'd lose a couple of appendages to frostbite while waiting. Before storming off, he screamed out, "Merit is subjective, and that's just plain unfair!"

Neither of them grew up in a rich family, but their perspectives on wealth couldn't be more different. He believes that the rich should pay a far bigger share in taxes and that there's such a thing as "making too much money." She feels that the amount of money you make shouldn't determine the size of your contribution, and that it isn't the job of the government to decide when you get shuffled into a "making too much money" bracket. I remember that their first big fight started because he was a little too amused by the fact that the very rich guy next door, who also happened to be her brother, had just lost his job.

Even the act of arguing itself—subject matter aside—was a problem. He found her "too judgmental." She felt he was "never able to see a clear right versus wrong." It went on. And on.

And so I'm left wondering … can two people walk through life side by side who see the world so differently? After all, politics isn't just some memo you read, fold up, and forget about until the next morning. Your views on national security, immigration, abortion, government, gun rights … they all come together to create the bigger picture of who you are and what you value. If two people's bigger pictures are diametrically opposed, can they live happily ever after? And if opposites do in fact attract, are we all just a bunch of masochists?

Okay, that's enough philosophy for one day. It's time for a cookie break. Right after I stop laughing about that fight I had a couple of years ago with an old boyfriend because he was offended by my U.S. Army t-shirt. Good grief. Masochist, indeed.

* * * * *

I thought I'd share some of the conversations I had with students and/or overheard at school today.

This one took place after I handed out blank maps of the United States and asked students to fill in the names of states that have a large Spanish-speaking population:

Student 1: I don't know what half of these states are.

Student 2: Me, neither.

Me: What do you mean? You guys don't know the states?

Student 1: Well, I know the important ones.

Me: The important ones?

Student 2: Yeah, like California and New York.

Me: So, what constitutes an unimportant one?

Student 1: Well, you know. No one cares about Idaho. Or Kansas. Give me a break.

Student 2: Yeah, kind of like Alaska. That's like hardly a state.

This occurred after an in-class debate kids were having in Spanish:

Student: Honestly, Ms. Bila, I don't mean to be rude. But I'm sort of surprised that you teach Spanish.

Me: Why?

Student: Well, you're a Republican. And, no offense, but we all know Republicans don't like other cultures.

As kids were packing up at the end of class, I had this exchange with a student:

Student: Ms. Bila, I shouldn't have gotten a B.

Me: Well, you left out five questions.

Student: I deserve an A anyway.

Me: No, you earned a B.

Student: I studied for like four hours. I'm *entitled* to an A.

I overheard this gem in front of school during my free period:

Student 1: My friend does this awesome Sarah Palin impersonation, way better than Tina Fey.

Student 2: Palin is such a dummy.

Student 1: I don't even think she went to a real college. Probably too dumb to get in.

Student 2: I know. Where do you want to go again?

Student 1: Yale.

Student 2: You've got the grades for Yale?

Student 1: No, but my dad's a donor.

It was saddening, but I quickly reminded myself of several students I'd taught who had been raised in families where they had to work hard to earn rewards, where they had learned that the parameters of the United States extend far beyond New York City and San Francisco. If they got a C, they asked what they could do to study better. They had been taught that their money doesn't define their character. And they didn't turn their noses up at those who didn't have fancy clothes, chauffeurs, or fifty-thousand dollar birthday parties. Interestingly enough, the politics of the parents of those two very different groups of kids were often strikingly different as well.

There's nothing worse than kids who grow up thinking that their parents' money will pave the way for their success. There's nothing better than those who are taught to work their tails off to make their dreams come true.

The majority of kids I've taught over the years harbor a wealth of misconceptions about everything from Republicans and Democrats to history and our Constitution. American ideals of personal responsibility and self-sufficiency are about as foreign to them as the Pledge of Allegiance and the lyrics of our national anthem. It's a scary thing to see. And it's even scarier to feel somewhat helpless to right those wrongs.

* * * * *

I stopped by the nail salon this afternoon on my way home from the drugstore. Why is it that I can never leave a drugstore with just the one item I went in for? Somehow it always turns into one absurd purchase after another. So, this time was no different. I entered the nail salon with my CVS bag in hand, filled with lip balm, three hair clips, some sort of exfoliating cream, a toothbrush, batteries, and a neon mini-flashlight. Oh, and the box of tissues I went in for.

There was a new young woman working whom I hadn't met. After speaking with her for a few minutes, I learned that she had arrived a few weeks prior from South Korea and that she had just turned twenty-five. Her English was shaky, but I admired her willingness to speak and her desire to practice, regardless of the mistakes she might make.

She asked me many questions about vocabulary and expressions, and her diligence with respect to pronunciation and grammar was impressive. She talked about America, about how happy she is to have the chance to be here, and about how many opportunities have already come her way. She was excited to

115

learn more English and curious about the ins and outs of our culture. Although her grandparents want her to return to South Korea, she hopes to start a business of her own in America one day.

"What is it like to grow up in America?" she asked.

"It's like being able to dream up all these dreams of what you'd like your life to look like, and know that you're in the best place to make them happen," I replied.

"You're lucky to have been born here," she said. "But I'm also lucky to be here now."

"You're not that lucky," a woman interjected as she stood up and retrieved her designer purse. "America has plenty of flaws. We could stand to be a little less war-hungry. And half the country is ass-backwards." She hurried out, holding a cell phone in each hand.

Today wasn't the first time I'd spoken to a young, industrious immigrant who was grateful to be in America and who, without having spent much time in our country, had already grasped its exceptionalism. It also wasn't the first time I'd witnessed a snooty American ingrate degrade our country while carrying some token of the wealth it enabled him or her to acquire.

I treasure people who come to this country with big goals, loads of ambition, and an inspiring work ethic. I thank them for the key role they play in enhancing the productivity and cultural beauty of our nation, and I appreciate the respect they have for our country, language, and culture. The young girl from South Korea in the nail salon today reminds me of a young gentleman from Russia I met last year at a downtown café. He had worked his way up to manager in two short years and would spend his lunch breaks studying the Oxford English Dictionary. I remember overhearing a tourist ask him what nationality he was. "American," he answered proudly.

I have little patience for Americans who berate the country that has afforded them opportunities so many would die for. I have even less patience for elitists who disparage certain states, our military, or some combination of the two. And I'm all for encouraging those who don't appreciate what makes America exceptional to hop on a plane or swim on over to somewhere they'd like better.

* * * * *

I went to The Metropolitan Museum of Art after work today.
There's just something about museums that takes my mind off of
everything. The rows of colors, shapes, and textures launch me
into worlds so different from the one I'm used to, and I love it.
Not to mention the fact that on a good day, I can draw a
mediocre stick figure. So, my fascination with artists and their
skills is no secret. Yes, it has gotten me into my fair share of bad
first dates. No, I haven't been entangled in a wild love affair with
an artist who swept me off my feet in a studio in Soho, where he
spent countless hours painting the silhouettes of his lost loves.
Wait, what was I talking about again?

Anyway, I was standing in one of the Impressionist rooms
taking notes on the qualities I was drawn to. I've always
preferred my paintings somewhat blurry and imprecise, with
visible brushstrokes that make the artist's presence that much
more tangible. As I scribbled down some descriptive adjectives, a
woman interrupted me.

"You can't be serious with that?" she asked. I was perplexed at first, then noticed her pointing to the "Drill, Baby, Drill" sticker on my journal.

"Quite, actually," I answered.

"Have you no regard for the environment?"

"Plenty," I said.

"In this day and age, it's hard to imagine that people like you still exist. I guess you don't care about clean air, either. Do you not read *The New York Times*?"

"Actually, I love clean air," I replied. "I have to admit, though, I'm not a big fan of *The New York Times*." She looked horrified.

"Well, you should read it. You obviously have a lot to learn." She stormed off.

I tried not to laugh too loudly, but it was tough. The notion that right there, in the midst of such incredible art, a stranger had felt the need to confront me about a sticker, was far too entertaining. I could almost hear her telling her friends that she had met some whack job in the museum who is pro-drilling. And who isn't a fan of *The New York Times*. Ghastly, I say.

I went on to explore for another hour or so. I was, of course, mesmerized by a handful of artists who were sketching in front of paintings, so I spent much of the time trying to stare at their hands without seeming like a stalker. It was no small task.

As I sat outside on the museum steps, I caught a glimpse of the woman who had been so bothered by my sticker. She tossed a rolled-up piece of aluminum foil onto the sidewalk, lit up a cigarette, and spit out her gum on the street. Now if only I could learn to have such "regard for the environment."

* * * * *

I went to a lounge tonight on the Upper West Side for my friend's birthday. By the time I arrived, she had already downed three cosmos and was crying because her sort-of-boyfriend had spent the first hour talking to a half-naked bartender. He's been a jerk since day one, but she has a thing for bad boys and there was no talking her out of it.

I spent some time mingling with her friends, all of whom tried to convince her to leave the bad boy and give a nice guy a chance. No such luck. She and her bad boy made up shortly after. About ten minutes after he apologized, I overheard him asking her if he, she, and the bartender could work something out. I really, really wish I was kidding.

I stepped out briefly with a friend of hers to grab a bite to eat. I hadn't had time for dinner and was famished. (I can be a little dramatic when it comes to food withdrawal, but if you ever have the chance to be in my company after I've missed a meal, we'll all agree it's best that I always stay well-fed.) He and I sat at a café, quickly ordered, and got to talking. He's a wealthy businessman and will one day inherit his dad's company. He talked about his "impressive salary" and four-bedroom apartment. He's also a political junkie and big-time Obama supporter.

He didn't take too well to my opposition to Obama's ideology or my conservative values, and he initially entertained himself with jokes about my "simple" Staten Island upbringing. The crux of our disagreement emerged with respect to his support for—and my distaste for—wealth redistribution. He argued passionately for it, saying that it's the duty of the wealthy to give their "excess money" to the less fortunate. I voiced my support for charitable donations over government manhandling of one's money. We went back and forth for about fifteen minutes. Neither of us convinced the other of anything.

When it was time to pay the bill, he grabbed the check, looked it over, and placed just enough money down to cover his meal. I paid for my share. He also placed a five-dollar bill on the table for the tip, stood up, and walked away. I added the extra necessary five. I later found out that he had given my friend a whopping twenty-five dollars as a birthday gift.

What's that saying again? Oh, right. "Do as I say, not as I do."

* * * * *

An acquaintance invited me for drinks at a Houston Street lounge tonight. Just as I was about to agree, she said this: "Oh, but one thing. You may have to ignore my friend if he calls you a racist. He was next to me the last time you and I were on the phone talking about how you don't like Obama. He went on this rant about how you're a racist. So if he brings it up, just ignore him."

"What?" I replied. "I'm not going to ignore him if he says something ridiculous like that. Are you kidding me?"

"Ugh, God. What's the big deal? I mean, who really cares?" she asked.

"I do. And the big deal is that it's not true."

"Well, then maybe you shouldn't come," she said.

"What? Hold on, are you telling me that if I can't keep my mouth shut if and when someone calls me a racist, I shouldn't come?"

"I'm just saying that you could easily just let it go," she answered.

I suppose that some might wonder why I couldn't just ignore it all and go about my business, enjoying a night out. And maybe with something different, I could have. If he had just called me a jerk or a nerd or made fun of my clothing, I wouldn't have cared one bit. However, this race game when it comes to Obama has to stop. And it's not just about Barack Obama.

Our world is becoming a very scary place, one in which you can't criticize someone's policies because you will immediately be called racist, gender-biased, or some other convenient label. And I'm not about to play that game. I appreciate the historical significance of electing an African-American man to the presidency, just as I would appreciate the historical significance of electing a woman to the presidency. However, I don't believe that the gender and/or race of politicians should be a factor in determining my support for them. I'd hope that President Obama, despite our ideological differences, would agree with me on this one.

My friend, the one who asked me kindly to zip my lips if and when I'd be called a racist, phoned me around 9:00 p.m. to say that the coast was clear, that the guy who may have been inclined to call me a racist hadn't shown up, and that I should come down and join the party. I felt that a simple "No thank you" on my part sufficed. I wasn't angry at her, but she still didn't get it. I hope that someday she will.

I capped off the evening chatting on the phone with a friend, who jokingly called me a racist every twenty seconds or so just to amuse himself. He's Puerto Rican, African American, and Caucasian, and didn't vote for Obama. I guess that makes him a racist, too.

Jedediah Bila

* * * * *

I spent some time this morning reading the news and returning emails. I was also temporarily fascinated by a coat rack online in the shape of a giraffe, but I digress.

I signed on to Facebook shortly after and began surfing around. Three of my former professors belonged to a few interesting groups: "1,000,000 Strong Against Sarah Palin," "Can this poodle wearing a tinfoil hat get more fans than Glenn Beck?," and "One Million Shoes for George W. Bush." As always, the diversity of thought in academia was inspiring.

As I browsed their pages, I noticed that many of their current and former students were their Facebook friends. What a great message to send to your students—that it's acceptable, if not downright commendable, to throw a shoe at a sitting United States president. I thought the academic elite were supposed to represent the pinnacle of sophistication? Oh, wait. That's only when they agree with you.

I started to think about my experiences in academia. I remembered a professor who told me bluntly that he felt it was his job "to help students see things the right way." It also

126

happened to be the socialist way. I remembered the anti-Bush hate speech that rolled off the tongues of some of my graduate school classmates on a regular basis.

I remembered hearing some of my teaching colleagues stand up in assemblies and declare that "Reaganomics didn't work" and that "vouchers are unfair" (a mind-boggling position for a teacher in a private school where tuition is more than $30,000 a year). Such teachers got rounds of applause from the students who had come to believe they were right. I remembered those same teachers smiling ear to ear when students put on an election skit that depicted Sarah Palin as a first-class idiot.

I also remembered the administrator who had been excited about an upcoming conference our students might attend because Al Gore would likely be speaking there. When another teacher announced in a meeting that she thought Sarah Palin might be there as well, the room was full of gasps and the administrator replied with, "I certainly hope not." Once again, there had been no regard whatsoever for the fact that someone in that room might not agree. And if they couldn't fathom that *I* might be sitting there with a different opinion, what about the kid in the third row of their classrooms? Did he or she have a chance?

I won't deny that I'm sometimes scared for the future of this country. How can I not be, when I've heard countless stories over the years about the Pledge of Allegiance being thrown under the bus and politically correct rewritten history being glorified?

I spent tonight sitting at a coffee shop, drinking tea and reading a novel that transports me away from my reality when I need it most. Three college students nearby were discussing a possible thesis topic, "a rebuke of America's imperialist ways." One of them had this written on her backpack: "Europe is like America, only smarter."

I couldn't begin to imagine the kinds of courses that had encouraged the ideology they now espouse. And I couldn't help but feel disgusted by the tendency of so many members of our youth to be ingrates, to have no appreciation for the country that affords them the freedom to criticize it so. I can't help but wonder if there's a bigger role I can play in all this, a bolder way to remind our youth what America stands for and why she's so exceptional.

March 2009

* * * * *

I had lunch with an acquaintance at her newly-renovated apartment on the Lower East Side. Although it's a small space much like mine, she had situated the furniture in a way that lent a lovely, open vibe to the studio. She had made delicious veggie tacos, a salad, and some sort of dessert with apples and oats that I couldn't get enough of. We talked about anything and everything, and it wasn't until the end of our conversation that I realized just how different we actually are.

She started by insisting that *someone* needs to put her on a diet before she eats her way into a size ten. I replied that *I* need to get myself into a better workout routine, as I'm feeling more tired than I should.

She talked about how she had just spent $5,000 on furniture she can't afford. I talked about how I need a bunch of things that will just have to wait, as I don't have the cash.

She spoke about how she feels *entitled* to more money from her job at a day care center because kids are tough work. I agreed that kids are tough work, and said that I hope to have the chance to prove myself more and *earn* a higher standing at my school.

She talked about how she's had a hard time quitting smoking and wishes the government would hike up cigarette taxes so she'd be unable to afford the nasty habit. I talked about how my grandfather, who smoked a pack a day for twenty years, looked me in the eye as a kid and made the decision to quit so he might live to see me grow up. He never picked up a cigarette again.

She spoke about how she feels like we're always fighting an unnecessary war. I spoke about how grateful I am for those standing on the front lines so that I could sit at her house and enjoy my third taco.

She talked about how sad it is that people walk around carrying guns like it's nothing. I talked about how scary it would be to live in a world where criminals do that every day, but she and I couldn't.

It wasn't until I finished my last statement that I fully understood how one's conservative or liberal makeup is woven throughout his or her approach to just about everything. And it wasn't until this afternoon that I began to truly absorb why my conservative friend and her liberal husband had been unable to build a life together.

Someone once told me that conservatives and liberals are like apples and oranges. But when you think about it, apples and oranges aren't that much different. It's not apples and oranges. It's apples and airplanes.

* * * * *

"What the hell are you reading?" an acquaintance asked me as she peered over my shoulder. She had met me at Whole Foods to chat for a bit. "Oh my God, is that Rush Limbaugh?"

"Yeah, why?" I asked.

"I really hope you're not serious," she said.

"Why? What's the problem?"

"Just that he's the biggest piece of garbage that ever walked the face of the earth," she replied.

"Really? How so?"

"He just is."

"How so?" I repeated.

"He's the biggest hypocrite in the world."

"In what way?" I asked.

"He just is. He says one thing and does another."

"In what sense?"

"In every sense. He wants you to live one way, but it's okay for him to do what he wants."

"In what sense?" I repeated.

"In all senses."

As you can see, she was a little light on details. The conversation proceeded as such for a few minutes. She huffed, puffed, and rolled her eyes. She intermittently inserted "Goddamn hypocrite" and "Piece of shit hypocrite" into the mix. She finally let it go and began talking about the environmental studies program she was engaged in and how it's imperative that we save the world "one tree at a time."

She spoke at length about global warming, about America's obsession with consumption and how it's eating away at our resources. She talked about how much Al Gore has done for the betterment of our country and how Rush Limbaugh could stand to learn a few things from him. She looked confused when I suggested that Limbaugh could learn from Gore how to spew global warming fables from the comfort of a private jet or a mansion that likely uses more energy in a month than I do in a year.

Tonight I stopped by a party she was hosting at her apartment in the Village. To be honest, I wasn't in a partying mood, but another friend promised that if I spent an hour there with her, she'd give me the three homemade artichokes her mom had made. I considered it a worthwhile trade.

Upon entering her two-bedroom apartment, I noticed that almost everyone was smoking. A stereo and a muted television were on in the living room. A light was on in both vacant bedrooms. The bathroom had a gadget plugged in that gave the illusion of a running waterfall. A curling iron and a blow dryer were also plugged in. I was amused beyond measure—an environmentalist after Al Gore's own heart.

It's around midnight now. I'm proud to say that I'm in full-on artichoke ecstasy. I'm off to do some writing before bed. But not before getting a little extra laughter at the thought of my Rush Limbaugh-hating acquaintance writing her environmental studies thesis amid more active electricity than Home Depot's lighting department.

* * * * *

While picking up veggies and wraps for dinner, I tried my best to ignore some anti-American babble by two women in line at the health food store. It began with the evils of President Bush and included a tribute to socialism. On the bright side, I noticed another woman nearby roll her eyes in response to the Bush-bashing. When it was just the two of us left at the counter, she whispered, "Enough is enough. He was no gem, but I think we're in for a lot worse." That was certainly a first for me in Manhattan. It was about time.

I spent a good part of the afternoon reading "news" articles. The more I read, the more disgusted I became. The state of objective media is an outright disgrace.

I sat for a while thinking about the election of 2008 and about what an Obama presidency would probably look like (still hoping I'd be dead wrong). I picked up some of my personal writings, none of which I intend to publish. Some secrets of your soul are meant to stay that way. I moved on to folders filled with research papers on art, literature, and philosophy. *That's a lot of time*, I thought. And then I glanced over at a couple of political reflections I'd written over the past few months.

I suddenly felt lost and didn't know why. And then I remembered something that seemed to pop up out of nowhere, something a college professor told me twelve years ago. I had been sitting in his office talking about how I didn't know what to major in, how I had no idea where I was headed or how I'd get there. I remember him removing his glasses—he had the perfect professor spectacles—and saying, "You're a writer, whether you like it or not. If you ever feel lost, just sit down, trust it, and write." I don't know why that memory came to me in that moment, but I know that a political column flowed rather quickly from my "pen" soon after.

And so a new chapter begins.

IV.

OLD BUDDY, OLD PAL AND SCHOOLHOUSE GRACE

March 2011

* * * * *

Well, it has certainly been an interesting two years. I guess you could say that my focus on writing political commentary was born in March of 2009. My columns were soon featured in *Human Events*, *The Daily Caller*, and the Association of Mature American Citizens' newsletter. I launched a website in December of 2009—JedediahBila.com—and radio and television appearances soon followed.

I can now be found calling it like I see it weekly via columns and on a variety of programs, as well as on Facebook and Twitter. I feel blessed to have the chance to contribute on television and radio to important political and cultural discussions, and to sit beside the likes of Sean Hannity, Stuart Varney, and so many respected voices. I feel honored to have readers and subscribers who support my writing, offer wonderful commentary, and make me laugh when I need it most. I am thankful for the opportunity to meet so many courageous political figures and to have had the honor of conducting a telephone interview with Governor Sarah Palin, who I've also had the privilege of meeting in person.

In a nutshell, I followed my heart—as always—and have held dear the wise words of my former college professor to "sit down, trust it, and write" when I feel lost. It never disappoints me.

It's safe to say that my life has changed a bit since the time frame of this text began. It's also safe to say that some around me haven't been quite so happy about it. Let's start with some of my New York City "friends"—you know, the ones who decided that my weekly columns and/or television appearances were "too much to handle." I had one tell me that we could continue being friends as long as she'd never have to read my "mean writing." Another asked me how I wasn't ashamed to live in such a "diverse, accepting city like New York" and harbor such "deviant, abnormal views." I'll let you re-read that one a few times before moving on.

An old boyfriend came out of the woodwork to say he'd like to date me again, but only if he would never have to watch me on TV. He was as charming as ever. An instructor at the gym now refers to me as "the conservative" in the class. He usually follows it up with a statement on why he's a Democrat. Others who work at Manhattan spots I often frequent and know of my recent ventures have stopped me to comment on how George W. Bush or Sarah Palin is a "dummy."

Some in the school where I taught were exceptionally thrilled as well. (Ahem.) Here's a sample of some of the comments, exchanges, and happenings that came my way before I resigned from my position in the summer of 2010:

> "You don't look like a conservative. I mean, you're not wearing a Walmart t-shirt." That comment from an administrator cracked me up for days, as did his later remark that, "Your best friend couldn't possibly be a conservative. He just looks so liberal."

> "It's a good thing or you might get assaulted," said an administrator in response to me stating that I'd like my

school life and outside political life to remain separate. He was joking, but may have had a point.

From an administrator: "Give me a heads up when you'll be on *Hannity* next so I can watch," followed by "I can't stand Sean Hannity. He's such a hypocrite and a liar."

After my first *Hannity* appearance, a student's friend stopped me outside of school to ask if I was "a racist, a homophobe, or a little of both."

Two parents and one administrator thanked me for my Fox News work and columns. They were whispering and frantically looking around while they spoke, so as to ensure that no one was coming and/or could hear them. I felt like I was part of a top-secret investigation, which I enjoyed. I made a mental note to purchase a Sherlock Holmes hat, which I was convinced would make me look significantly cooler. Regardless of their tiptoeing and whispering, they appreciated my message. And that counted for a whole lot.

I found out at some point that another teacher had published an article in a well-known liberal publication.

He had even photocopied it and passed it out to some of his classes. I spent several hours thoroughly entertained by the reactions that would've ensued had I handed out my "Palin's Bull's-Eye in the Big Easy" column.

My awards for the "Best 'Tolerant' Liberal Quotes from the Spring of 2010" go to ... drumroll ... an acquaintance who said, "Conservatives are like acid because they burn the good stuff away"—yes, she may have been on acid—and a teacher at school who ran around the faculty room repeating the line, "If Palin becomes president, I'm moving to Mexico to become an illegal immigrant." Enough said.

In many ways, my life as a conservative living in Manhattan is just as it has always been. One thing has changed, though—I got a Maltese! Her name is Emma and she is my world. I named her after that adorable little girl I encountered outside who had been briefly separated from her mom. Remember the one who complimented me on my American flag pin? I have to say that it's truly amazing how much eight pounds of white fluff can brighten your day. And yes, of course, my Emma has a conservative wardrobe to die for.

Bottom line: Maybe I have a little bit more of a platform these days, but I'm still just a regular Manhattan conservative. And to the liberal New York City elite, public enemy #1.

Jedediah Bila

V.

EPILOGUE

May 2011

* * * * *

A very wise woman once told me something I'll never forget. She's my Aunt—Aunt Ro Ro, as I used to call her. She's not a blood relative, but she's one of my mom's best friends and was right by my side through the first eight or so years of my life.

Rose and I were sitting on the beach in Florida one night. I was polishing off a large vanilla ice cream cone and Rose was sitting beside me with her usual hefty stack of napkins.

I remember seeing a woman who used to walk the beach around dinnertime. She was probably around forty or so, wore the brightest and boldest clothing ensembles, and would walk her two cats on leashes. She had a high-pitched voice and would sing Boz Scaggs's "We're All Alone" over and over again, night after night. Sometimes she'd sit on a beach chair nearby and whisper those same lyrics, looking out at the sunset. Our neighbors said she believed that angels walk the earth beside us and that God talks to us through flowers and waterfalls.

One day, she passed by us with her cats as I was spilling the last of my ice cream on my Wonder Woman t-shirt. "Great t-shirt," she said as she smiled at me. I didn't reply and looked away.

When she was far off in the distance, Rose turned to me and asked, "Why didn't you answer that lady?"

"Because she's creepy," I said. "She dresses funny and talks to herself."

"She's not creepy. She's just different from you and me," Rose replied. I was entirely unconvinced. "Don't make that mistake," she said. I sat up and paid attention, as I often did when she spoke. And I'll never forget the essence of what followed. Of course, I can't remember it word for word. But here it is, as I recall it:

"You're going to meet a whole lot of different people in your life. Some will have voices that sound different from anything you've ever heard. And some will think differently. They'll look at the same thing you're looking at and see something completely different. Don't ever miss the chance to get to know someone simply because that person sees things differently from you. Life's too short to write people off like that. If you do, you might miss something great."

I didn't fully understand her words that night, and Rose didn't expect me to. But she knew that one day I would. Her advice that evening helped to shape the way I've lived my life. I remembered it when I made my first middle-school best friend. She and I couldn't have been more opposite. And I remembered it the first time I fell in love … with someone who saw so much of the world so differently than I did. In fact, it was on a tough drive home from visiting that first love that I remember listening to "We're All Alone" over and over. Maybe that "creepy" woman on the beach and I had something in common after all.

So I sit here now, staring out my Manhattan window as I often do, watching taxis pass by and people stroll around on this beautiful New York City night. I'm not thinking about all the episodes that created this text. And I'm not focused on the few "friends" I've parted ways with as I've ventured on this journey with an unknown destination.

I'm thinking about Rose. I'm realizing that perhaps that's where my fondness for the wisdom of older generations was born—right there on the beach that night. And I'm thanking her for planting the seed that has helped me to embrace the most unlikely of companions. I'm also getting a full-on kick out of the fact that so many of my lefty "friends"—you know, the ones who labeled me racist and intolerant—would be flabbergasted by the fact that my Aunt Rose, who helped to raise me beside my parents, is a Puerto Rican lesbian.

Some will wonder why I chose to publish this text. I did so because I saw something—a pattern, a motif—that embodied an importance far beyond me or New York City. The 2008 presidential election is behind us, but many of the themes illuminated in these pages by the voices of the liberal Manhattan elite are alive and well. In fact, just this past month alone, I've overheard comments about how "Sarah Palin's violent rhetoric caused the Tucson killings," how "Barack Obama hasn't had enough time to fix that idiot Bush's mess," and how "Republicans are undermining our president because they are hateful racists." Sadly, times in my beloved Manhattan haven't really changed.

With 2012 rapidly approaching, it's perhaps more important than ever for people to take a moment to self-reflect … to do their research … and to be the independent thinkers that could build a real hub of diversity like the one Manhattan claims to be.

There's no integrity in hypocrisy. There's no honor in casting someone as the enemy simply because it's what you've been trained to do. There's no truth without honest debate. And words like "feminism," "tolerance," and "diversity" cease to have meaning when they're touted by those whose actions exemplify their opposites.

If you're a true champion of diversity, you'll appreciate that woman or man in the room who doesn't see the world the way you do. Heck, you might even be brave enough to take a step into his or her world, open your eyes, and look around. I've done so many times. It has given me a stronger sense of who I am and a stronger commitment to the conservative values I hold dear, but it has also given me an immense respect for the right of people to disagree with me. And a passion to defend their right to do so.

I don't feel it's my job to tell you what to glean from the journey I've shared on these pages. I'd prefer for you to discover whatever you may through the uniqueness of your very own lens. And I thank you so very much for walking with me.

Good night, all. I'm off to catch up on some news, kiss Emma about three-hundred times, and likely burn my dinner.

Oh, and to write a column. Like I always say, let the games begin.

Jedediah Bila

VI.

ACKNOWLEDGMENTS

Thank you to God for guiding me, listening to my anxious rants, and helping me to never lose sight of the fact that through it all, you're right by my side.

Thank you to my parents for your endless wisdom and for continuing to put up with my impatient, perfectionist tendencies. You are my anchor.

Thank you to Emma and Bronte, my two loves, for reminding me what's important when I need it most. You have given my life so much meaning.

Thank you to my two best friends, Mike and Lauren, for making it so much fun to laugh at myself every day. I am so grateful for your input, feedback, and advice. I love you and will likely have spoken to each of you twice before I finish writing this section.

Thank you to Mike Rigal for your beautiful photography. Talent is talent, my friend.

Thank you to Mark R. Levin for paying tribute to my writing way before it was featured in any fancy publications. It has been a true honor to have your support. I will never cease to admire your intellect, love of country, and call-it-like-you-see-it approach.

Thank you to Sean Hannity for your kindness and for being the first to invite little old me to hit TVs across the country. I have immense respect for your work ethic, commitment, and patriotism.

Thank you to David Limbaugh for your generosity, advice, and encouragement. Your work and your wisdom are an inspiration to me.

Thank you to Tammy Bruce for your support, kindness, and thoughtfulness. Your vitality and wit never cease to amaze me.

Thank you to John Gizzi for being one of my biggest supporters since day one and for coining the term "Bila groupie"! You are living proof that it's possible to thrive in D.C. and keep your soul intact.

Thank you to *The Daily Caller*, *Human Events,* and the Association of Mature American Citizens for welcoming my written words, as unconventional as they often are.

Thank you to Greg Gutfeld, Andy Levy, and Bill Schulz for keeping me laughing. Love you guys!

Thank you to Conservatives4Palin for consistently paying tribute to my writing. I have great respect for the investigative work that you do.

Thank you to the Majabra team for all of your hard work. A very special thanks to my web designer, webmaster, and book cover designer, Maura, for the incredible amount of patience you've had when dealing with me—no small task, to say the least. Your talent inspires me.

Thank you to Manhattan, without which this text would have never been born. You may think I hate you, but you're wrong. Much like all things I love so dearly in this world, I want you to be the best that you can be. Learning to embrace not-so-common conservatives like me will make you brighter, bolder, and tomorrow's leader.

And, from the bottom of my heart, thank you to all of my readers and subscribers. It is *you* who inspire me to grow, to persist, and to write. I am so grateful for your encouragement and your thought-provoking and often-hilarious emails, tweets, and Facebook comments. I am honored to stand beside you in this fight—relax lefties, it's just an expression—to bring America back home.

—Jedediah

Jedediah Bila

VII.

PHOTO GALLERY

Emma Bila

Jedediah Bila

"Me on July 4, 2009, after being schooled by 'The Great One.' I later told a liberal bulldog to 'Get off my block, you big dope!'"
—*Emma*

Jedediah Bila

"Dreaming about a conservative victory. And about how to snag a seat on the Great, Great, Great American panel."—*Emma*

"David, you had me mesmerized! I say we co-author the next one together. Tentative title: *Conservative Twitter King and Reaganesque Pup Take D.C. by Storm.*"—*Emma*

156

"Michelle, I took a bite out of corruption! (I also may have swallowed a small portion of your cover, but I digress.)"—*Emma*

"That's right, folks. Every now and then I go rogue."—*Emma*

"Nothing like a lazy Sunday afternoon with a mama grizzly.
P.S.—Sarah, where's my moose stew?"—*Emma*

VIII.

ABOUT THE AUTHOR

Jedediah Bila is a conservative columnist and commentator. She contributes to *The Daily Caller*, *Human Events,* and the Association of Mature American Citizens' newsletter. She is a regular guest on Fox News and Fox Business, including such programs as *Hannity*, *Fox & Friends*, *Red Eye w/ Greg Gutfeld*, *Varney & Co.*, and *America's Nightly Scoreboard*, among others. She has also been a guest on MSNBC and talk radio. Jedediah graduated Valedictorian of Wagner College and earned a Master of Arts degree from Columbia University. She lives in Manhattan with her two-year-old Maltese, Emma. For more information on Jedediah, please visit www.jedediahbila.com.

12645363R00096

Made in the USA
Charleston, SC
18 May 2012